easy everyday
Air Fryer
77 simple and delicious recipes
for beginners and experts alike
LOVE FOOD™

Contents

Vegetarian

Dessert

Introduction

Welcome a new, life-changing appliance to your kitchen: the air fryer! Deep frying yields deliciously crispy and decadent foods, but it leaves a heavy smell. Some even fry outside in the freezing cold just to keep the odors out. Deep frying also saturates food in fat, which makes it an unhealthy option for everyday cooking. The air fryer is a healthy cooking tool that eliminates that frying smell. It makes super crispy french fries, but also other products such as potato croquettes and ground-meat sausages come out nicely crisp on the outside and still soft on the inside.

The Healthy Alternative

Many dishes you would normally prepare in the deep fryer, oven, or pan taste just as good when cooked in the air fryer—and require significantly less fat. Take, for example, a breaded chicken tender. You would need about a half stick of butter to get that golden brown and crispy crust in a frying pan. That's not exactly ideal when it comes to healthy cooking! Air-fried breaded chicken tenders are extra crunchy and stay moist inside, using just a bit of fat. Meatballs turn a beautiful golden brown, and the fat that drips off the meat ends up in the bottom tray to be discarded. This drastically reduces your intake of fat!

More Benefits

The air fryer makes cleaning a breeze. With a little hot water and a drop of dish soap, the bottom tray is fresh and clean in no time. The optional racks, baskets, and grill plates only need a quick scrub. And all the removable components are dishwasher safe. How could it be any easier? The air fryer is preheated in just a few minutes and therefore very energy efficient.

Are there any cons about an air fryer? Yes, there are some: Air fryers have a limited basket capacity, so if need be, cooking is done in multiple batches. But in that case, when one batch is ready, simply sit down at the table while the second batch is cooking in the air fryer. By the time you've finished the first batch, the second one is ready. It's just a matter of good planning.

Highly Versatile

Air fryers are for more than just french fries and snacks. You can also grill, roast, caramelize, and bake in the air fryer. This book will show you how to use your air fryer for pretty much any meal of the day in a range of cuisines from around the world. It's no wonder the air fryer has quickly become an indispensable kitchen gadget!

All about Air Fryers

Home air fryers were introduced for the first time in France in 2006. Their major breakthrough in Australia and Europe came in 2010, followed by Japan and the United States. Since then, the demand for air fryers has continued to grow. Even those who are not cooking fanatics are intrigued by this promising new gadget.

Air fryers and convection ovens use similar techniques. By circulating hot air at high speed, the heat is distributed evenly over the food from all sides. It is this technique that gives food the delicious crisp edges that make it seem like it has been deep-fried.

As the trend for air frying caught on, numerous manufacturers perfected their own machines. As a result, air fryers are now available in various makes and models.

If you are looking to buy your own air fryer, it is a good idea to find out which type best suits your needs. These are the factors you need to bear in mind: size, ease of use, how it needs to be cleaned, design, availability of accessories, and, of course, cooking results.

One thing is certain, the air fryer is a must-have in every contemporary kitchen. It fits in perfectly with the trend of fast, easy, and healthy. And air fryers can do a lot more than just frying. You can cook just about anything you would normally prepare on the stove top or in an oven in the air fryer. The possibilities are endless, so the air fryer is here to stay.

Air-Fried Meat and Fish

Virtually any type of meat and fish you can cook or barbecue is suitable for the air fryer: sausages, steak, ham off the bone, satay, tenderloin, chops, salmon, cod, sardines, trout, shrimp, you name it. Best of all, the fat drips out of the food as it cooks in the air fryer. Lean meat, such as beef or chicken fillet, can be brushed with a little oil to give it more color. The heat is distributed evenly in the air fryer, so there's no need to flip meat or fish as it cooks.

Most kinds of meat can be cooked at 350°F. If you want to sear meat, like steak, you can start at 400°F, then lower the temperature to 350°F after a few minutes.

Meat or fish is cooked in the same amount of time as it takes in a pan to prevent it from burning. An exception are thick types of meat, such as ham off the bone or a roast. As the interior needs to be properly cooked as well, this takes a little more time. The same goes for whole fish. Start at 350°F to ensure that the meat or fish is cooked all the way through. When a flavorful crust is formed on the outside, lower the temperature to 300°F and maintain it until the meat or fish is done on the inside.

If necessary, use a meat thermometer. Insert the tip into the thickest part of the meat to check for doneness.

Baking in the Air Fryer

Air fryers are perfect for baking pies or cakes because they basically use the same cooking method as the convection oven but take less time and energy to preheat. As well as baking pans specially designed for air fryers, any baking pan or oven dish that can withstand temperatures up to 400°F is suitable for the air fryer. You will still need to grease the pan first and preferably place a sheet of parchment paper on the bottom. This will make it easier to turn out the pie or cake after baking.

It may help to place the baking pan directly on the bottom of the air fryer, so you can use a slightly larger size. To prevent the pan from scratching the coating, place three silicone muffin cups upside down on the bottom to support the pan. This will keep the air fryer scratch-free while giving you that extra space!

Similar to a traditional oven, the pie or cake should not come out undercooked. The indicated cooking time is always a guideline and may vary slightly between air fryer models. Doneness is also influenced by the amount of batter and the size of the baking pan. Check if the pie or cake is done by opening the air fryer toward the end of cooking and by inserting a skewer into the center. If it comes out clean, your pie or cake is ready!

Cooking Time Chart

The general cooking times below apply to various potato products, fresh vegetables, and all kinds of meat and fish. The cooking times are guidelines and may vary among air fryer makes and models.

TIPS

- For best results, always preheat the air fryer. This takes about 2 minutes.
- Do not place the items against each other in the air fryer basket.
- Shake the basket a few times to prevent sticking and to ensure even browning.
- Check the food regularly for doneness during cooking.

Potatoes

Potato Cubes	400°F	6 minutes
Potato Slices	350°F	12 minutes
Baby Potatoes	400°F	14 minutes
Potato Croquettes	350°F	12 minutes
Potato Wedges	400°F	12 minutes
Hash browns	400°F	14 minutes
French Fries	350°F	12 minutes

Vegetables

Cauliflower Florets	400°F	14 minutes
Broccoli Florets	350°F	10 minutes
Zucchini Slices	400°F	8 minutes
Kohlrabi Cubes	350°F	8 minutes
Bell Pepper	350°F	12 minutes
Snow Peas	350°F	5 minutes
Sugar Snap Peas	400°F	5 minutes
Fennel Strips	400°F	8 minutes
Carrot Slices	400°F	6 minutes

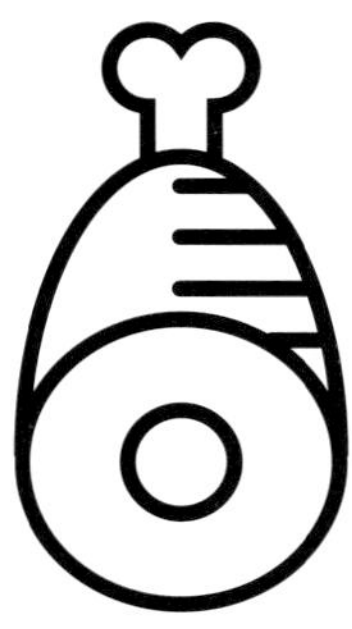

Meat

Steak, Medium	400°F	8 minutes
Meatloaf Logs	350°F	15 minutes
Bratwurst	350°F	12 minutes
Cordon Bleu	350°F	10 minutes
Hamburger	350°F	8 minutes
Chop	350°F	8 minutes
Chicken Fillet	350°F	8 minutes
Chicken Nuggets	400°F	8 minutes
Chicken Satay	400°F	6 minutes
Croquette	350°F	10 minutes
Lamb Chop	350°F	7 minutes
Beef Sausage	350°F	11 minutes
Sausage Roll	350°F	5 minutes
Shawarma	350°F	10 minutes
Pork Tenderloin	350°F	18 minutes
Rolled Pork Roast	325°F	45 minutes

Fish

Calamari	325°F	10 minutes
Trout (Whole)	325°F	15 minutes
Cod	350°F	8 minutes
Alaska Pollock	300°F	6 minutes
Fried Fish	350°F	12 minutes
Tilapia Fillet	350°F	9 minutes
Shrimp	350°F	5 minutes
Salmon	350°F	7 minutes
Sea Bass (Whole)	350°F	18 minutes
Fish Fingers	350°F	10 minutes

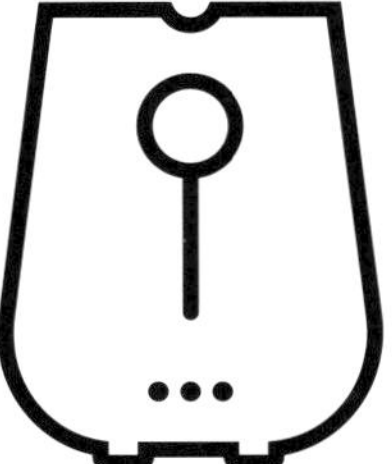

good
morning!
wake
up!

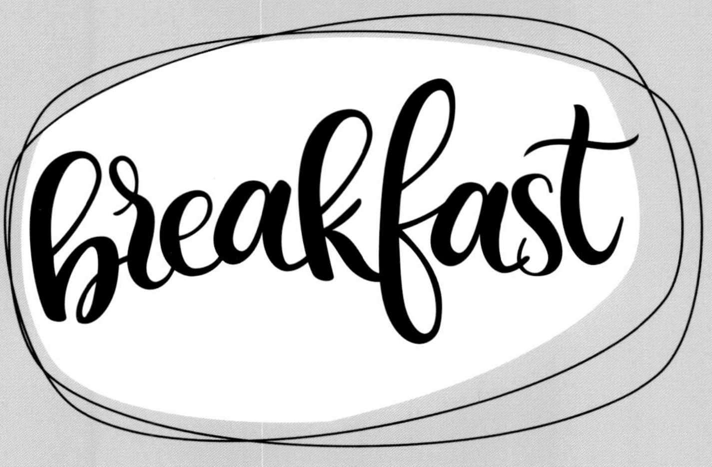
breakfast

granola
with yogurt and blueberries

INGREDIENTS TO SERVE 4

for 5 cups of granola

- ¼ cup / 2 fl oz coconut oil
- 1 cup rolled oats
- ½ cup pumpkin seeds
- ½ cup sunflower seeds
- ¼ cup / 2 fl oz honey
- ¼ cup brown sugar
- 2 tbsp cinnamon
- ½ cup dried cranberries
- ⅔ cup goji berries

for the yogurt

- 2 cups / 16 fl oz Greek yogurt
- ½ cup granola
- 1 cup fresh blueberries
- ¼ cup / 2 fl oz honey

Making granola in your air fryer is super easy, and you can safely store leftovers in an airtight container.

STEP 1

Melt the coconut oil in a saucepan over medium–low heat. Add the oats, pumpkin seeds, and sunflower seeds. Then add the honey, brown sugar, and cinnamon. Stir until well combined. Remove the basket from the air fryer and preheat to 325°F. Line the basket with parchment paper or use a baking tray that fits into the air fryer. Distribute half of the granola evenly over the parchment paper. Bake for about 20 minutes, turning occasionally, until golden brown and crunchy. Spread the granola evenly over a cool baking sheet, then bake the remaining granola the same way. Allow both batches to cool, then stir in the dried cranberries and goji berries.

STEP 2

Divide the yogurt between 4 glasses. Sprinkle the granola and blueberries on top. Drizzle with honey, or serve it separately.

banana bread
with walnuts and salted caramel

INGREDIENTS TO MAKE 1 LOAF

for the banana bread

- 2 ripe bananas
- 2 eggs
- 6 tbsp / 3 fl oz sunflower oil
- ¼ cup sugar
- 1¼ cup self-rising flour
- 1 tsp ground cinnamon
- ½ tsp ground cloves
- ¾ cup walnuts, coarsely chopped

for the salted caramel sauce

- 1 cup sugar
- ½ cup / 4 oz butter, cut into cubes
- ½ cup / 4 fl oz heavy cream
- 1 tsp coarse sea salt

STEP 1

Mash the bananas and beat in the eggs. Mix together the sunflower oil and sugar, then stir in the banana mixture. Add the flour, ground cinnamon, ground cloves, and half of the walnuts, then stir until a smooth batter is formed. Remove the basket from the air fryer and preheat to 325°F. Grease a round or wide rectangular baking pan that fits into the air fryer.

Spoon the batter into the pan, and bake the banana bread for 15–20 minutes. Remove the bread from the pan and transfer to a wire rack to cool.

STEP 2

To make the salted caramel sauce, heat the sugar with ¼ cup / 2 fl oz water in a heavy-bottomed saucepan over medium heat until the sugar is completely melted. Leave the sugar mixture to simmer. Do not stir, but move the pan around occasionally. Once the sugar begins to color, add the butter over low heat. Allow the butter to melt. Carefully add the cream, a little at a time, still over low heat. Briefly bring the mixture to a boil and leave to simmer for 1 minute. Remove the caramel from heat and add the salt. Allow the caramel to cool. Pour caramel over the banana bread until it is covered, and sprinkle the rest of the walnuts on top. Serve the remaining caramel separately.

oatmeal crumble

with fruit filling

INGREDIENTS TO SERVE 1

- 1 tbsp / ½ fl oz coconut oil
- 1 tbsp / ½ fl oz honey
- 1 tbsp sunflower seeds
- 1 tbsp pumpkin seeds
- ½ cup oats
- 1 cup soft fruit (blueberries, raspberries, or cherries)

Oatmeal is high in fiber, lowers cholesterol, and contains antioxidants. Best of all, it keeps the hunger away. The combinations with oatmeal are endless. For a great start to your day, you can easily turn it into a tasty and filling breakfast, like this fruit crumble. And by adding a scoop of vanilla ice cream, this crumble becomes a delicious dessert.

STEP 1

Melt the coconut oil in a saucepan over medium–low heat. Add the honey, sunflower seeds, pumpkin seeds, and oats. Stir until well combined. Arrange the fruit in an oven-proof dish that fits in the air fryer basket, and sprinkle the crumble on top.

Preheat the air fryer to 350°F, and bake the fruit crumble for 5 minutes, or until the fruit is bubbling and the oatmeal has turned golden brown.

coconut rolls

INGREDIENTS TO MAKE 7

- 2 cups self-rising flour, plus extra for dusting
- ½ tsp sea salt
- ½ cup shredded coconut
- 1 tbsp honey
- 1 cup / 8 fl oz coconut milk
- butter, for greasing
- powdered sugar, to decorate

STEP 1

Put the flour, sea salt, shredded coconut, and honey in a bowl, then mix until well combined. Make a well in the middle and slowly pour in the coconut milk, stirring the dough until it comes together.

STEP 2

Lightly dust the work surface with flour, and turn out the dough. Knead for 5 minutes until smooth. Return the dough to the mixing bowl, cover with a kitchen towel, and leave to rise for 1 hour at room temperature.

STEP 3

Preheat the air fryer to 350°F. Line the basket with parchment paper and grease with butter. (Alternatively, grease a round or rectangular pan that fits into the air fryer basket.) Turn the dough back onto the work surface. Divide it into 7 equal portions, and form each portion into a ball. Place one ball in the center of the basket and arrange the remaining 6 balls around it. Bake the rolls in the air fryer until golden brown and crispy, about 30 minutes. Sprinkle with powdered sugar just before serving.

oatmeal patties
with cranberries and pumpkin seeds

INGREDIENTS TO MAKE APPROX. 15

- 2 large ripe bananas, peeled and sliced
- 1 cup quick-cooking oats
- 1 tsp ground cinnamon
- ½ cup dried cranberries
- ⅓ cup dried pumpkin seeds

STEP 1

Puree the bananas with a hand mixer or finely mash them with a fork. Stir in the oats. Then add the ground cinnamon, cranberries, and pumpkin seeds, and stir until combined. Cut parchment paper to the size of the air fryer basket. Drop two-tablespoon size portions of the mixture onto the paper. Use the back of the spoon to shape and flatten the patties.

STEP 2

Preheat the air fryer to 350°F. Bake the patties in batches of 5. Bake until golden brown, about 10–12 minutes.

pumpkin bread

INGREDIENTS TO MAKE 1

- 1 medium-sized pumpkin
- 3 eggs
- ⅔ cup / 2½ oz cream cheese
- 1½ cup buckwheat flour
- ½ cup almond flour
- ½ cup dried pumpkin seeds
- 3 tsp honey
- 2 tsp baking powder
- 1 tsp salt
- 2 tsp Chinese five-spice powder

STEP 1

Preheat the air fryer to 325°F. Cut the pumpkin in half, or chunks small enough to fit in the air fryer, and remove the seeds. Cover the cut side of each pumpkin half with aluminum foil, and bake in the air fryer for 50 minutes. Scrape out the pumpkin flesh and process in a food processor until smooth. Measure ½ cup of mashed pumpkin, and set aside the remaining pumpkin for another recipe.

STEP 2

Increase the air fryer temperature to 350°F. Beat the eggs with a mixer until fluffy, then beat in the mashed pumpkin and cream cheese. In a separate bowl, mix together the buckwheat flour, almond flour, dried pumpkin seeds, honey, baking powder, salt, and five-spice powder. Fold the mixture with a spatula into the pumpkin mash and stir to form a smooth batter. Transfer the batter to a greased round or wide rectangular baking pan that fits into the air fryer and bake the bread in the air fryer for about 1 hour.

This will be magic

fish

fish burgers

with bacon, radishes, and lemon mayonnaise

INGREDIENTS TO SERVE 4

for the lemon mayonnaise

- 1 lemon
- ¼ cup / 2 fl oz mayonnaise

for the fish burgers

- 2 slices white bread
- 1 lime
- 7 oz smoked salmon
- 7 oz smoked trout
- 1 green onion, finely chopped
- 1 egg
- pinch of pepper and sea salt
- 4 ciabatta rolls
- 8 bacon slices
- 1 bunch radishes
- ¾ cup lettuce

STEP 1

Zest the lemon and juice one lemon half. Combine the lemon zest and juice with the mayonnaise.

Process the white bread in a food processor to fine breadcrumbs, remove from food processor, and set aside. Zest and juice the lime. Add the salmon, trout, green onion, lime zest and juice, egg, pepper, and sea salt to the food processor. Process until the mixture reaches a coarse consistency, then transfer to a bowl. Add the breadcrumbs, and knead until well blended. Form the mixture into four patties.

STEP 2

Preheat the air fryer to 350°F. Cut the ciabatta rolls in half and grill in the air fryer for 3–4 minutes. Cook the bacon in the air fryer until crispy, about 5 minutes. Bake the fish burgers in the air fryer for 8 minutes.

STEP 3

Set 4 radishes aside and thinly slice the rest. Spread the rolls with the lemon mayonnaise, and place the lettuce on top. Then add the fish burgers and top with the bacon, lemon mayonnaise, and sliced radishes. Put the top halves on the rolls. Garnish the burgers with a radish and wooden skewer.

Serving tip: steam fresh snow peas in the air fryer and serve with the fish burger.

Serving tip:
serve mashed
(sweet) potatoes
and ratatouille
(see page 128)
with the
fish fillet

tilapia fillets
with garlic, lemon, and thyme

INGREDIENTS TO SERVE 4

- ¼ cup / 2 fl oz olive oil
- 1 tsp fish sauce
- 1 lemon, zested and sliced
- 1 tsp paprika
- pinch of coarsely ground pepper
- 1 garlic bulb
- 8 cleaned tilapia fillets
- coarsely ground pepper
- 4 tomatoes, sliced
- 2 orange bell peppers, sliced into rings
- a few sprigs of fresh thyme, finely chopped
- sprig of fresh basil, finely chopped

STEP 1

In a bowl, mix together the olive oil, fish sauce, lemon zest, paprika, and pepper. Peel the garlic bulb. Crush 2 garlic cloves over the bowl and stir until well blended. Rub the tilapia fillets with the marinade, and leave to marinate for about 2 hours.

Cut parchment paper into eight 15 x 15 inch pieces. Place a marinated tilapia fillet on each piece. Place the remaining garlic cloves on the fillets, and sprinkle with ground pepper. Distribute the lemon, tomato, and bell pepper slices over the packets, then drizzle the remaining marinade on top. Fold the parchment over to create packets, and secure them with cooking twine.

STEP 2

Preheat the air fryer to 350°F. Place the fish packets in the air fryer basket and cook for 8–10 minutes.

STEP 3

Just before serving, open the packets, and sprinkle the fish with fresh thyme and basil.

shrimp with rice noodles
in coconut milk with Thai seasoning

INGREDIENTS TO SERVE 4

- 5 oz rice noodles
- 16 oz peeled large shrimp (about 30–36 medium)
- 1 tbsp olive oil
- 1 cup broccolini
- 2 garlic cloves, minced
- 1 red pepper, finely chopped
- 1-inch ginger root, peeled and grated
- 1 lemongrass stalk, coarsely chopped
- ½ tsp curry powder
- ¾ cup / 6 fl oz coconut milk
- salt and pepper, to taste

STEP 1

Cook the rice noodles according to the package instructions, and keep warm.

STEP 2

Preheat the air fryer to 400°F. Toss the shrimp with olive oil in a heat-proof bowl that fits in the air fryer. Place the bowl in the air fryer and cook for 5 minutes. Add the broccolini, garlic, pepper, ginger, lemongrass, and curry powder, toss to combine, then cook for an additional 5 minutes. Pour in the coconut milk and stir until well blended.

STEP 3

Combine the shrimp with the rice noodles. Season with salt and pepper, and serve immediately.

piri-piri shrimp
with soba noodles and broccolini

INGREDIENTS TO SERVE 4

- 24 large shrimp
- 8 red and/or green chilies
- pinch of salt
- 4 garlic cloves
- ¼ cup / 2 fl oz olive oil
- ⅓ cup / 3½ fl oz lemon juice
- 5 oz soba/buckwheat noodles
- ¾ cup broccolini
- 1 tbsp flat-leaf parsley, coarsely chopped
- 1 tbsp sesame seeds

STEP 1

Remove the head of the shrimp and pull out the vein. Cut 1 red and 1 green chili into rings and set aside. Add the rest of the chilies, salt, and garlic to the food processor and process until combined and finely chopped. Add the olive oil and lemon juice, then process to a thick sauce. Coat the shrimp with the sauce, and leave to marinate in the refrigerator for 30 minutes.

Cook the soba noodles according to package instructions. Cook the broccolini in lightly salted water until tender but still firm to the bite, about 3 minutes. Drain the broccolini and combine with the noodles.

STEP 2

Preheat the air fryer to 350°F. Put the shrimp with the sauce in an heat-proof dish that fits into the air fryer, and cook for 6–7 minutes, turning the shrimp occasionally.

STEP 3

Divide the noodles with the broccolini between the plates, and arrange the shrimp on top. Sprinkle with the red and green chili rings, chopped parsley, and sesame seeds.

salmon with pesto
and cherry tomatoes

INGREDIENTS TO SERVE 4

- 4 salmon fillets, about 5 oz each
- 3 tbsp green pesto
- salt and pepper, to taste
- 1 lb spaghetti
- 16 oz cherry tomatoes (about 15–20)
- 1 tbsp toasted pine nuts
- 1–2 tbsp olive oil
- fresh basil, to garnish

STEP 1

Preheat the air fryer to 350°F. Spread 2 tablespoons of pesto over the salmon fillets, and season with salt and pepper. Place the fillets in the basket and bake for 8 minutes.

STEP 2

Cook the spaghetti al dente on the stove top according to package instructions. Cut the cherry tomatoes in half. Drain the spaghetti, and mix in the cherry tomatoes, and pine nuts. Combine the remaining pesto with the olive oil, and mix into the spaghetti.

STEP 3

Divide the spaghetti between warmed plates, and place a piece of salmon on top. Garnish the fish with fresh basil.

SERVING TIP

Serve with an arugula salad with extra cherry tomatoes, pine nuts, and Parmesan cheese.

cod

with za'atar and toasted nuts

INGREDIENTS TO SERVE 2

- ¾ cup raw almonds
- ¾ cup raw hazelnuts
- 2 sprigs of parsley
- ¼ cup grated parmesan cheese
- 1 tsp za'atar seasoning
- salt and pepper, to taste
- 2 cod fillets

STEP 1

Preheat the air fryer to 350°F. Put the almonds and hazelnuts in a heat-proof bowl, and toast in the air fryer for 5 minutes. Watch closely to make sure they don't burn. Allow to cool slightly.

STEP 2

Strip the parsley leaves off their stems. Add the toasted almonds and hazelnuts, the parmesan, za'atar seasoning, parsley, and salt and pepper in the food processor and pulse until finely chopped and combined. Pat the cod fillets dry, and sprinkle with salt and pepper. Place the fillets in the heat-proof bowl, and press the nut mixture firmly onto the fish.

STEP 3

Preheat the air fryer to 350°F. Bake the cod fillets for 6–8 minutes, until the crust is golden brown and the cod is cooked through.

SERVING TIP

Serve the cod with a Lebanese fattoush salad. Toast a few pita breads and cut into pieces. Make a dressing of olive oil, lemon juice, sumac (a Middle Eastern spice), and salt and pepper. Mix together cucumber chunks, radish slices, cherry tomato halves, little gem salad strips, and minced fresh mint, then pour the dressing on top. Garnish the salad with pieces of toasted pita bread.

grilled avocado

with egg and salmon

INGREDIENTS TO MAKE 4

- 2 avocados
- 4 eggs
- salt and pepper, to taste
- 3½ oz smoked salmon
- 4 sprigs of flat-leaf parsley, finely chopped
- 1 lemon, cut into wedges

STEP 1

Cut the avocados in half lengthwise, and remove the pit. Use a spoon to slightly widen the hole where the pit was, and cut a thin slice from the bottom so the avocado will lay upright. Crack one egg into each hole and season with salt and pepper.

STEP 2

Preheat the air fryer to 400°F. Place the stuffed avocados in the basket and bake for about 15 minutes, until the yolk reaches the desired consistency.

STEP 3

Place the avocados on a dish and distribute the smoked salmon on top. Sprinkle with parsley, and squeeze the lemon wedges over the top.

SERVING TIP

Serve the grilled avocado with toasted bread and a fresh green salad.

grilled sea bass

with stewed vegetables and herbs

INGREDIENTS TO SERVE 2

- 2 sprigs of parsley
- 2 sprigs of thyme
- 2 sprigs of rosemary
- 1 onion, diced
- 1 yellow bell pepper, diced
- 1 red bell pepper, diced
- 1 orange bell pepper, diced
- 1 green bell pepper, diced
- ½ zucchini, diced
- 3 garlic cloves, minced
- 2 tbsp olive oil
- salt and pepper, to taste
- 2 small sea bass fillets
- 1 lemon, sliced

STEP 1

Remove the parsley and thyme leaves from their stems. Strip off the rosemary needles. Finely chop the herbs. Mix the vegetables with the garlic and herbs, stir in the olive oil, and season with salt and pepper.

Using a sharp knife, make small cuts about 1 inch apart in the skin of the sea bass. Fill the sea bass with lemon slices and some of the vegetable-herb mixture.

STEP 2

Preheat the air fryer to 350°F. Place a heat-proof bowl in the air fryer, add the fish, and spoon the rest of the vegetable-herb mixture onto the fish. Cook for 10–12 minutes.

STEP 3

Serve the sea bass on a bed of vegetables.

SERVING TIP

Sea bass combines perfectly with unpeeled, boiled baby potatoes.

loaded potato skins

with tomato salsa, salmon, and sour cream

INGREDIENTS TO MAKE 4

- 2 large potatoes
- 2 tomatoes, diced
- 5½ oz shredded salmon
- 20 sprigs of fresh chives, finely chopped
- 6 sprigs of fresh parsley, finely chopped
- salt and pepper, to taste
- 2 tbsp grated parmesan cheese
- 2 tbsp sour cream

STEP 1

Scrub the skin of the potatoes and pat dry. Preheat the air fryer to 400°F. Pierce the potatoes with a fork a few times, place them in the basket, and bake for 25 minutes. Remove the potatoes from basket and allow to cool for 10 minutes.

STEP 2

In the meantime, combine the tomatoes with the shredded salmon. Keep some of the chives and parsley aside for garnish, and stir the rest into the tomato-salmon mixture. Season with salt and pepper.

Cut the potatoes in half lengthwise and hollow each half out. Mash the potato flesh and mix it with the tomato-salmon salsa. Fill the hollow potatoes with the salsa, and sprinkle the parmesan cheese on top.

STEP 3

Return the filled potatoes to the air fryer and cook for another 2–3 minutes. Then place the potatoes on a dish, scoop a spoonful of sour cream on top, and garnish with the remaining chives and parsley.

fish burgers
with shrimp and avocado cream

INGREDIENTS FOR 4 ROLLS

for the fish burgers

- 1 lb cod
- 7 oz small cooked shrimp
- 1 egg
- 1 bunch cilantro
- 2 garlic cloves
- pinch of freshly ground pepper and salt
- mild olive oil

for the avocado cream and serving

- 1 lime
- 2 avocados
- ¾ cup / 6 oz mascarpone cheese
- 1½ tsp dill
- 1 round loaf of bread, cut into thick slices
- alfalfa sprouts

STEP 1

Put the fish, half of the shrimp, egg, most of the cilantro, garlic, and salt and pepper in a food processor. Keep some cilantro aside for garnish. Pulse briefly, and shape the minced fish into 4 large burgers. Preheat the air fryer to 350°F. Place the fish burgers in the basket and bake in the air fryer until golden brown and crispy, about 10 minutes.

STEP 2

Zest and juice the lime. Cut the avocados in half, remove the pit, and scoop out the flesh with a spoon. Blend the avocado, mascarpone, dill, and lime juice and zest in the food processor to a smooth, creamy consistency. Spread the slices of bread generously with avocado cream, sprinkle with cilantro, and top with a fish burger, extra avocado cream, alfalfa, and shrimp. Cover with a slice of bread and secure with a pick.

mini quiches

with smoked salmon and asparagus

INGREDIENTS TO SERVE 4

- 7 oz asparagus (7–10 spears)
- 4 puff pastry slices
- 2 oz smoked salmon, cut into pieces
- 1 tbsp capers, coarsely chopped
- 2 sprigs of dill, minced
- butter, for greasing
- 2 eggs
- ½ cup / 4 fl oz heavy cream
- salt and pepper, to taste

STEP 1

Chop off the ends the asparagus. Cook on the stove top in lightly salted water for 3 minutes, then drain.

STEP 2

Preheat the air fryer to 400°F. Grease 4 mini tart or quiche pans with butter. Lightly roll out the puff pastry to fit the pans, press the pastry firmly into the pans, and trim the edges. Place a piece of parchment paper onto the bottom of the pastry, and cover with pie weights or dry beans. Bake the pastry in the air fryer for about 8 minutes. Depending on the size of the pans, you need to do this in 1 or 2 batches. Remove the pie weights or beans, and bake the bases for another 5 minutes. Lower the temperature of the air fryer to 325°F.

STEP 3

Distribute the salmon, asparagus, capers, and dill over the pastry bottoms. Beat the eggs. Whip the cream with a little salt and pepper into the egg mixture, then pour over the filling. Bake the quiches in the air fryer until the filling is set, about 20 minutes.

grilled fish
with orange

INGREDIENTS TO SERVE 4

- 2–4 small whitefish
- 5 garlic cloves, grated
- 1-inch piece of fresh ginger root, grated
- 2 oranges
- 1 tsp cumin
- 2 tbsp sesame oil
- 1 bunch fresh cilantro, finely chopped
- 2 limes
- 4 bay leaves
- pepper and sea salt, to taste

You can use any kind of whitefish for this recipe, such as tilapia, trout, or cod. To check for the freshness of fish, look at the eyes: If they are clear, the fish is fresh; if they are cloudy, don't buy it. Ask the butcher or grocer to clean the fish.

STEP 1

Score the fish, leaving about 1 inch between cuts. Add the grated garlic and ginger to a mortar. Zest and juice 1 orange over the mortar. Add the cumin and sesame oil, then finely grind. Coat the fish with the marinade.

STEP 2

Place half of the cilantro inside the belly of the fish, and sprinkle the rest on top. Cut the remaining orange and limes into slices. Fill the fish with the citrus slices and bay leaves, then sprinkle with freshly ground pepper and sea salt. Preheat the air fryer to 400°F. Lightly grease the air fryer basket with oil. Place the fish in the basket and bake until done, about 15 minutes. Depending on the size of the fish, you can bake them all together or in 2 batches. Remove the bay leaves before serving.

SERVING TIP

Serve with couscous with fried eggplant and zucchini.

sole rolls

stuffed with shrimp, mussels, and squid in white wine sauce

INGREDIENTS TO SERVE 4

- 8 sole fillets
- salt and pepper, to taste
- 12 oz mixed seafood (fresh or frozen)
- 1½ sticks / ¾ cup cold butter, diced
- bunch fresh carrots, peeled
- 1 cup / 8 fl oz fish broth
- ½ cup / 4 fl oz vermouth
- ¼ cup / 2 fl oz dry white wine
- ½ cup / 4 fl oz heavy cream
- 1 tbsp finely chopped parsley

STEP 1

Pat the sole fillets dry, and sprinkle with salt and pepper. Roll up the fillets, leaving room for the seafood. Secure each roll with a toothpick. Preheat the air fryer to 350°F. Line the air fryer basket with parchment paper, and place the sole rolls upright in the basket. Fill them with the mixed seafood and top with a tablespoon of butter. Bake the fish in the air fryer for 6–8 minutes.

STEP 2

Cook the carrots on the stove top in lightly salted, boiling water for 4–5 minutes.

STEP 3

Bring the fish broth, vermouth, and white wine to a boil on the stove top, then let reduce to ⅓. Add the cream, and let reduce again by half. Beat in the remaining cold butter and cream, then stir in the parsley. Place the carrots and sole rolls on a plate, and top with the sauce.

air-fried sardines
with caramelized onions

INGREDIENTS TO SERVE 4

for the sardines

- 16 sardines
- extra-virgin olive oil
- coarsely ground pepper, to taste
- coarse sea salt, to taste

for the caramelized onions

- 2 onions, thinly sliced
- mild olive oil
- ½ cup / 4 fl oz Marsala wine
- 1 tsp thyme
- 1 tsp cinnamon
- ¾ cup pine nuts
- ½ cup raisins

for serving

- 4 sprigs of fresh parsley
- extra virgin olive oil

STEP 1

Preheat the air fryer to 400°F. Lightly grease the air fryer basket with oil. Place the sardines in the basket. Drizzle with extra-virgin olive oil, and sprinkle with pepper and sea salt. Bake the sardines in the air fryer for about 10 minutes.

STEP 2

Heat some olive oil in a pan and fry the onions on the stove top, about 5 minutes. Add the Marsala, thyme, cinnamon, pine nuts, and raisins, then stir-fry for 5 minutes.

STEP 3

Serve the sardines with the caramelized onions, and garnish with parsley and some extra virgin olive oil.

SERVING TIP

Serve with flatbread and a fresh fennel salad.

baked potatoes

with guacamole and salmon

INGREDIENTS TO MAKE 8

- 8 small unpeeled potatoes
- ½ cup / 4 fl oz heavy cream
- 2 sprigs of fresh dill or chives
- 1 avocado, finely mashed
- 10 sprigs of cilantro
- pinch of coarsely ground pepper
- sea salt, to taste
- 7 oz shredded smoked salmon
- 1 lime, cut into wedges
- 1 red chili pepper, thinly sliced into rings

STEP 1

Preheat the air fryer to 400°F. Scrub the skin of the potatoes and pat dry with paper towel. Place the potatoes in the air fryer basket and cook for 25 minutes until completely done. Insert a skewer into the potato. If it goes all the way through, the potato is ready. If not, return to the air fryer for another 5 minutes.

Mix together the heavy cream, dill, 2 sprigs of cilantro, avocado, pepper, and sea salt. Refrigerate the guacamole.

STEP 2

Remove the potatoes from the air fryer using kitchen tongs, and cut a crosswise slit in the top with a sharp knife. Gently squeeze the base of the potatoes to open them up. Just before serving, spoon a generous dollop of guacamole on the potatoes and sprinkle the shredded salmon on top. Garnish the potatoes with cilantro sprigs, lime wedges, and chili pepper.

calamari

INGREDIENTS TO SERVE 4

- 2 tbsp coarse sea salt
- 4 calamari, tubes cut into rings and tentacles left whole
- 2 limes
- ¼ cup / 2 fl oz olive oil
- 1 red chili pepper, sliced
- 2 garlic cloves, crushed
- 1 bunch parsley, finely chopped
- 1 bunch chives, finely chopped

STEP 1

In a bowl, mix 4¼ cups / 36 fl oz water and 1 tablespoon of sea salt. Put the calamari in the bowl and leave to rest, chilled, for an hour. Then cut into rings about ¼-inch wide.

Zest and juice 1 lime in a bowl. Add the olive oil, chili pepper, garlic, half of the parsley and chives, lime juice and zest, then stir until well blended. Mix the calamari with the herb oil and refrigerate for a few hours.

STEP 2

Preheat the air fryer to 400°F. Place enough calamari to cover a baking pan that fits into the air fryer. Cook in batches for 8 minutes, turning the calamari occasionally.

STEP 3

Sprinkle the remaining chives, parsley, and 1 tablespoon of sea salt over the calamari. Cut the remaining lime into wedges and garnish on top.

Thai fish balls

INGREDIENTS TO MAKE APPROX. 12

- 1 lb whitefish fillet
- 1 egg
- 1 mango
- 1 green onion, finely chopped
- zest and juice of 1 lime
- 1½ tsp red curry paste
- a few sprigs of cilantro, finely chopped
- salt, to taste
- ½ cup grated coconut

STEP 1

Cut the whitefish into pieces, and puree together with the egg in the food processor. Transfer the fish mixture to a bowl. Clean the mango and puree in a food processor. Spoon the mango, green onion, lime zest and juice, curry paste, and cilantro into the fish mixture, then season with salt. Form the mixture into 12 balls, and roll each ball in the grated coconut.

STEP 2

Preheat the air fryer to 400°F. Place the balls in the air fryer basket. Bake the fish balls until golden brown and crispy, about 7 minutes.

SERVING TIP

Serve the Thai fish balls directly from the air fryer with lime slices and sweet chili sauce.

Eat what you LOVE

Meat

A quick
and easy
recipe!

beef tenderloin

with blue cheese and grilled fig

INGREDIENTS TO SERVE 4

- 4 beef tenderloin steaks
- olive oil
- pepper and sea salt, to taste
- 5 oz blue cheese, cut into thin slices
- 4 fresh figs, cut in half

STEP 1

Bring the steaks to room temperature. Preheat the air fryer to 400°F. Rub the meat with olive oil and sprinkle with pepper and sea salt. Cut the cheese into thin slices.

STEP 2

Place the steaks with the fig halves in the air fryer basket. Grill the steaks on both sides for 5 minutes, 2½ minutes per side, until golden brown and crispy. For the last minute, top each steak with a slice of cheese and allow to melt slightly.

STEP 3

Serve the steak with the cheese and figs on a board.

SERVING TIP

Serve a fresh green salad and baked potatoes with the steak. You can make baked potatoes in the air fryer before cooking the steak. Scrub the potatoes and pat dry with paper towel. Place the potatoes in the air fryer basket, and cook at 350°F until done, about 25 minutes. Insert a skewer into the potatoes. If it goes in easily, the potatoes are done. If not, return to the air fryer for 5 minutes. Wrap the potatoes in aluminum foil to keep them warm.

rolled pork roast
with truffle sauce

INGREDIENTS TO SERVE 4

for the roast

- 1 garlic clove, crushed
- olive oil
- 1 tbsp honey
- 1 lb rolled pork

for the truffle sauce

- 7 tbsp / 3½ oz butter
- ¾ cup flour
- 1 cup / 8 fl oz mushroom broth
- 5 oz mushrooms, cut into quarters
- 1 tsp fresh thyme
- 1 tbsp truffle tapenade

for serving

- 4 sprigs of rosemary

STEP 1

Mix the crushed garlic with 2 tablespoons of olive oil and the honey. Spread the honey mixture evenly on the meat.

In a saucepan, melt the butter, and add the flour. Gradually pour in the mushroom broth, stirring until the sauce has thickened. Add the mushrooms to the sauce. Then add the thyme and truffle tapenade.

STEP 2

Preheat the air fryer to 325°F. Place the roast in the air fryer basket and bake for 45 minutes, turning occasionally until done. Use a meat thermometer to check for doneness. At an internal temperature of 145°F, the roast will be pink in the center. Remove from the air fryer, cover with aluminum foil, and leave to rest for 10 minutes.

STEP 3

Cut the roast into slices and serve with the truffle sauce. Garnish the meat with sprigs of rosemary.

Serving tip: delicious with white rice and stewed pears!

mashed pumpkin
with pancetta and mushroom wine sauce

INGREDIENTS TO SERVE 4

- 1 lb cooking pumpkin
- 2 garlic cloves, crushed
- ½ cup / 4 fl oz olive oil
- 2 tsp dried thyme
- 2 cups mushrooms, cut into quarters
- 3½ tbsp / 1¾ oz butter
- 1 tbsp flour
- coarsely ground pepper and sea salt, to taste
- ½ cup / 4 fl oz red wine
- ½ cup / 4 fl oz beef broth
- 8 pancetta slices
- 1 tsp fennel seeds
- ½ tsp nutmeg
- ½ cup / 4 fl oz heavy cream
- ½ cup / 4 oz mascarpone
- ½ cup / 4 oz stilton cheese, crumbled
- fresh rosemary
- fresh oregano

STEP 1

Peel the pumpkin, and cut into thin slices. Mix the crushed garlic with the olive oil and 1 teaspoon of thyme to create an herbal oil.

Fry the mushrooms in butter. Add the flour, 1 teaspoon of thyme, and salt and pepper. Gradually pour in the wine and broth. Stir the sauce until well blended.

STEP 2

Preheat the air fryer to 350°F. Place the pumpkin slices in the air fryer. Drizzle the herbal oil over the pumpkin slices and grill for 15 minutes, turning halfway through cooking. Remove the pumpkin from the air fryer.

Increase the temperature to 400°F, put the pancetta in the air fryer, and bake until crispy, about 5 minutes. Roll up the pancetta.

STEP 3

Transfer the grilled pumpkin to a bowl. Add the fennel seeds, nutmeg, cream, and mascarpone. Coarsely mash the pumpkin. Garnish the mashed pumpkin with crumbled stilton and sprigs of fresh rosemary and oregano. Briefly heat the mushroom sauce and serve the dish with the mashed pumpkin.

spare ribs
in maple syrup and beer marinade

INGREDIENTS TO SERVE 4

for the spare ribs

- ¼ cup brown sugar
- ¼ cup / 2 fl oz maple syrup
- ½ cup / 4 fl oz honey
- ¼ cup / 2 fl oz soy sauce
- ¼ cup / 2 fl oz pale ale
- 1 tsp coarsely ground pepper
- 1 tsp cinnamon
- 2 garlic cloves, crushed
- 1½ lb spare ribs

for serving

- sliced crusty bread

STEP 1

In a bowl, mix together the brown sugar, maple syrup, honey, soy sauce, pale ale, ground pepper, and cinnamon, and garlic. Place the spare ribs in the marinade and refrigerate for 2 hours.

STEP 2

Preheat the air fryer to 325°F. Cook the spare ribs for 30 minutes, until golden brown and crispy. Recoat the spare ribs every 4–5 minutes with the remaining marinade, turning occasionally.

STEP 3

Serve the spare ribs with crusty bread.

SERVING TIP

Serve with a tasty bean salad and precooked baby potatoes. Cook chopped green beans, lima beans, and sugar snaps in lightly salted water until al dente. Rinse the legumes under cold water and drain well. Mix with 7 oz cooked white beans, a finely chopped red onion, and a dressing of ¼ cup / 2 fl oz olive oil, 1 tbsp lemon juice, 1 tbsp honey, and salt and pepper. Mix until well blended. The baby potatoes can be served cold or briefly reheated so they are nice and warm.

Garnish the
bowl with
chili pepper
rings.

spicy meatballs

with edamame, bok choy, and ginger sauce

INGREDIENTS
FOR 2 BOWLS

- 1 red chili pepper, de-seeded and finely chopped
- 1 garlic clove, minced
- 1 tsp chili paste
- 2 tbsp sweet soy sauce
- 1 tsp ginger powder
- 6 oz ground beef
- 6 oz ground pork
- 1 egg
- 2 tbsp breadcrumbs
- 2 bunches baby bok choy
- 1 cup white rice
- ¾ cup / 6 fl oz ginger syrup
- 1-inch fresh ginger root, sliced
- ¼ cup shelled edamame beans, cooked
- salt and pepper, to taste

STEP 1

Mix together the chili pepper, garlic, chili paste, sweet soy sauce, ginger powder, ground meat, egg, and breadcrumbs, then knead everything together until evenly combined. Season to taste with salt. Form the mixture into small meatballs.

Cut the baby bok choy in half. Cook the rice until tender and keep warm. Bring the ginger syrup to a boil, then add the ginger slices. Leave the syrup to simmer for 8 minutes until thickened. Remove the slices, and season with salt and pepper.

STEP 2

Preheat the air fryer to 350°F. Place the bok choy halves in the air fryer basket and bake for 3 minutes. Remove the bok choy, place the meatballs in the air fryer basket, then bake for 8 minutes. Shake the basket twice during cooking to loosen the meatballs from the basket and to ensure even browning.

STEP 3

Divide the rice between the bowls, and top with the meatballs, bok choy, and edamame beans. Serve the ginger sauce separately.

babi kecap

marinated pork belly with sweet soy sauce

INGREDIENTS TO SERVE 4–6

for the meat

- zest and juice of 1 lime
- 1 inch fresh ginger, grated
- 2 garlic cloves, minced
- 1 tbsp brown sugar
- pepper and sea salt, to taste
- ¼ cup / 2 fl oz sweet soy sauce
- 1 tbsp honey
- 1 lb pork belly

for the sauce

- ¾ cup / 6 fl oz beef broth
- ½ cup / 4 fl oz sweet soy sauce
- ¼ cup / 2 fl oz apple or rice vinegar
- 2 tbsp ginger syrup
- ¼ cup brown sugar
- 2 garlic cloves, finely chopped
- 1 red chili pepper, de-seeded and finely chopped
- 1 inch fresh ginger, grated
- 1 tsp corn starch

STEP 1

Put the lime zest and juice, ginger, garlic, brown sugar, and a little salt and pepper in a mortar, then finely grind. Add the sweet soy sauce and honey, stirring until well blended. Spread the herb paste over the pork belly and refrigerate for at least 1 hour.

Preheat the air fryer to 350°F. Place the meat in an oven dish that fits into the air fryer and cook for 90 minutes. Turn the meat every 15 minutes for a crispy crust on all sides.

STEP 2

To make the sauce, bring the broth to a boil, then stir in the sweet soy sauce, rice vinegar, ginger syrup, brown sugar, garlic, chili pepper, and ginger. Leave the sauce to simmer for 10 minutes. Mix the corn starch with a few tablespoons of the warm sauce, then pour the mixture into the sauce. Keep stirring until the sauce thickens.

STEP 3

Remove the meat from the oven dish, and cut into slices. Arrange the slices on a dish. Pour the sauce over the meat to serve.

Tip: keep an eye on the baking process. If the meat turns too dark, lower the temperature of the air fryer to 325°F.

Garnish the iceberg lettuce with a red chili pepper and a sprig of chives.

satay with peanut sauce
and iceberg lettuce

INGREDIENTS TO SERVE 4

- 5 tbsp olive oil
- 1 red chili pepper, de-seeded and finely chopped
- 2 garlic cloves, minced
- juice of 1 lemon
- 2 tsp ginger powder
- ½ cup / 4 fl oz sweet soy sauce
- 1 tbsp ginger syrup
- salt and pepper
- 1¼ lb chicken fillet, cut into pieces
- 1 tbsp sugar
- ¾ cup smooth peanut butter
- 1 tbsp chopped peanuts
- 3½ oz iceberg lettuce

STEP 1

Make a marinade of the olive oil, red chili pepper, garlic, half of the lemon juice, 1 teaspoon of ginger powder, 4 tablespoons of sweet soy sauce, ginger syrup, and salt and pepper. Stir in chicken pieces and refrigerate for 30 minutes. Soak the skewers in water for 30 minutes. Thread the meat onto the skewers. Set aside the marinade.

For the peanut sauce, combine 1⅔ cup / 13¼ fl oz water with 3 tablespoons sweet soy sauce, 1 teaspoon of ginger powder, the remaining lemon juice, and sugar in a saucepan, and bring to a boil. Add the peanut butter and return to a boil, stirring gently. Keep stirring until the sauce is smooth. Pour marinade into the peanut sauce until it achieves the desired thickness. Allow the sauce to boil briefly. Sprinkle with the chopped peanuts.

STEP 2

Preheat the air fryer to 350°F. Place 3–4 satays in the air fryer basket. Bake in batches for 8 minutes, turning halfway through cooking.

STEP 3

Serve the satays with the peanut sauce and tufts of iceberg lettuce.

spicy meatloaf

INGREDIENTS TO SERVE 4

for the meatloaf

- 1 lb ground beef
- 1 red chili pepper, minced
- 1 green onion, chopped
- 1 tsp paprika
- 1 tsp mustard
- 3 tbsp breadcrumbs
- 1 egg
- salt and pepper, to taste
- olive oil, for greasing

STEP 1

Knead together ground beef, red chili pepper, green onion, paprika, mustard, breadcrumbs, egg, and salt and pepper. Grease a baking pan that fits into the air fryer, and evenly distribute the beef over the bottom. Smooth, and spread the top with olive oil.

STEP 2

Preheat the air fryer to 400°F. Place the baking pan in the air fryer, and bake the meatloaf for 25 minutes until golden brown and done. Cover and leave to rest for 10 minutes.

STEP 3

Remove the meatloaf from the pan, and cut into slices to serve.

SERVING TIP

Serve the meatloaf with a salad. Coarsely chop half a head of iceberg lettuce, cut a red onion into rings, and crumble a block of feta cheese. Mix the lettuce with the onion and feta cheese. Make a dressing of ¼ cup / 2 fl oz olive oil, 2 tbsp honey, 1 tbsp lemon juice, a pinch dried oregano, freshly crushed garlic, and salt and pepper.

Warm quiches are delicious for dinner. You can also eat them cold for lunch or as an appetizer.

quiche lorraine

INGREDIENTS
TO MAKE 12 MINI QUICHES

for the dough

- ½ cup / 4 oz cold butter, cut into cubes
- 2 cups wheat flour
- 1 egg
- pinch of salt

for the filling

- 4 eggs
- ⅔ cup / 5½ fl oz 2% milk
- 1 cup / 8 fl oz crème fraîche
- 1¼ cup grated parmesan cheese
- ¼ tsp nutmeg
- pepper, to taste
- 7 oz thick-cut smoked bacon, cut into ¼-inch strips

for garnish

- 2 tbsp flat-leaf parsley

STEP 1

Combine butter, flour, 1 egg, and a pinch of salt, then firmly knead by hand to an elastic dough. Cover the dough in plastic wrap and refrigerate for 1 hour. Roll out the dough on a floured work surface until ¼–⅛ inch thick. Grease 12 cupcake molds (choose a pan that will fit in the air fryer), then line with dough, cutting away any excess. Prick holes in the bottom of the dough with a fork.

In a bowl, whisk 4 eggs, then beat in the milk, crème fraîche, cheese, and nutmeg. Season to taste with pepper. In a frying pan, fry the bacon until crispy. Distribute the bacon over the dough bottoms, and pour the filling on top.

STEP 2

Preheat the air fryer to 400°F. Place a batch of the cupcake molds in the air fryer basket and bake until golden brown and done, about 25 minutes. Bake the rest of the mini quiches the same way.

STEP 3

Finely cut the parsley using scissors. Remove the quiches from the molds and sprinkle with parsley to serve.

Turkish pizza

with ground lamb and bell peppers

INGREDIENTS TO SERVE 4

for the dough

- 2 cups flour
- ½ tbsp dry active yeast
- 1 tsp salt
- ⅓ cup / 2½ fl oz milk
- 1 tbsp / ½ oz butter

for the filling

- 2 red bell peppers
- 1 tomato
- ½ red chili pepper
- 1 red onion
- 8 sprigs of parsley, finely chopped
- 5 oz ground lamb
- 1 tbsp tomato puree
- ½ tsp paprika
- 1 tbsp sunflower oil
- salt and pepper, to taste
- ¼ cup / 1⅓ oz crumbled goat cheese

STEP 1

Knead the flour, yeast, salt, milk, butter, and ⅓ cup / 2½ fl oz water into an elastic dough ball, cover, and leave to rise in a bowl for 45 minutes.

STEP 2

Chop 1 bell pepper, the tomato, red chili pepper, and onion, then finely process the vegetables with 4 sprigs of parsley in the food processor. Place the ground lamb in a bowl, add the ground vegetables, tomato puree, paprika, sunflower oil, and salt and pepper, and mix well with a fork.

Divide the dough into 4 equal portions and roll out each portion into an oval. pinch two opposite sides of the dough to create a boat-like shape. Finely chop the remaining bell pepper. Fill the pizza with the lamb mixture, and sprinkle the bell pepper cubes and goat cheese on top.

STEP 3

Preheat the air fryer to 400°F. Bake each pizza for 8–10 minutes in the air fryer. Sprinkle the pizza with the remaining parsley, and serve.

chicken souvlaki
with tzatziki

INGREDIENTS TO SERVE 4

for the souvlaki

- 1 tsp ground cumin
- 2 tsp paprika
- ¼ cup / 2 fl oz olive oil
- 1 tbsp vinegar
- salt and pepper, to taste
- 1¼ lb chicken fillet, cut into cubes

for the tzatziki

- ½ cucumber, grated
- 2 tbsp mint, finely chopped
- 2 garlic cloves, crushed
- 1 cup / 8 fl oz Greek yogurt

STEP 1

Mix together the cumin, paprika, olive oil, and vinegar. Add salt and pepper. Spoon in the chicken cubes and leave to marinate for at least 30 minutes. Soak skewers in water for 30 minutes, then thread the chicken onto the skewers.

To make the tzatziki, combine the cucumber, mint, cloves, and yogurt in a bowl.

STEP 2

Preheat the air fryer to 350°F. Place a batch of the souvlaki in the air fryer basket. Cook the souvlaki in batches for 8–10 minutes, turning occasicnally.

STEP 3

Serve the chicken souvlaki with the tzatziki sauce on the side.

SERVING TIP

Serve with bread and a Greek salad of cucumber, chopped beefsteak tomatoes, kalamata olives, red onion slices, olive oil, and feta cheese.

Mexican chicken wings
with salsa sauce

INGREDIENTS TO SERVE 4

for the chicken wings

- 2¼ lb chicken wings
- 1 tsp garlic powder
- 1 tsp onion powder
- 1 tsp dried thyme
- 2 tsp ground chili pepper
- 3 tsp paprika
- ½ tsp cayenne pepper
- pinch of salt

for the salsa

- 2 ripe tomatoes, finely chopped
- 1 shallot, finely chopped
- 2 tbsp lime juice
- 1 tbsp cilantro, finely chopped
- salt and pepper, to taste

for serving

- 1 tbsp sesame seeds
- 1 tbsp parsley, finely chopped

STEP 1

Pat the chicken wings dry. Mix together the garlic powder, onion powder, thyme, ground chili pepper, paprika, cayenne pepper, and a pinch of salt. Coat the chicken wings in the spice mixture.

To make the salsa, combine the chopped tomatoes and shallot with the lime juice and cilantro, then season with salt and pepper.

STEP 2

Preheat the air fryer to 350°F. Place a batch of the chicken wings in the basket; they may slightly overlap. Bake in batches until golden brown and done, about 20–25 minutes. Just before serving, return the chicken wings to the air fryer and heat for another 2 minutes.

STEP 3

Place the chicken wings on a serving plate, sprinkle with the sesame seeds and parsley, and serve with a bowl of salsa on the side.

tabbouleh salad
with Lebanese meatballs

INGREDIENTS TO SERVE 4

for the tabbouleh salad

- 1¼ cup couscous
- juice of 2 lemons
- ½ cup / 4 fl oz olive oil
- salt and pepper, to taste
- 7 oz red and yellow cherry tomatoes, halved (about 7–10)
- ½ bunch parsley, finely chopped
- ½ to 1 tbsp dried mint
- ½ cup mixed olives
- 2 oz feta cheese, cut into cubes

for the meatballs

- 1 lb ground beef
- ½ tbsp paprika
- ¼ tsp ground allspice
- 1 tsp ground cumin
- ½ tbsp mustard
- 1 egg
- 3 tbsp breadcrumbs
- salt and pepper, to taste

STEP 1

Leave the couscous to soak for 10 minutes in a large bowl of cold water. Line a strainer with a clean kitchen towel and put the couscous in the strainer. Gather up the towel's ends and twist to squeeze out the excess liquid. Transfer the couscous to a bowl and stir in the lemon juice and olive oil Season to taste with salt and pepper. Cut the tomatoes in half, then mix with the finely chopped parsley, mint, olives, and feta cubes into the couscous.

STEP 2

Knead the ground beef with the paprika, allspice, cumin, mustard, egg, breadcrumbs, and a little salt and pepper until well combined. Shape the mince mixture into 20 small meatballs.

Preheat the air fryer to 350°F. Place the meatballs in the air fryer basket and bake for 8–10 minutes. Shake the basket occasionally to loosen the meatballs from the basket until nicely browned on all sides.

STEP 3

Arrange the tabbouleh salad in a bowl and place the meatballs on top. Garnish the salad with lemon wedges and fresh parsley.

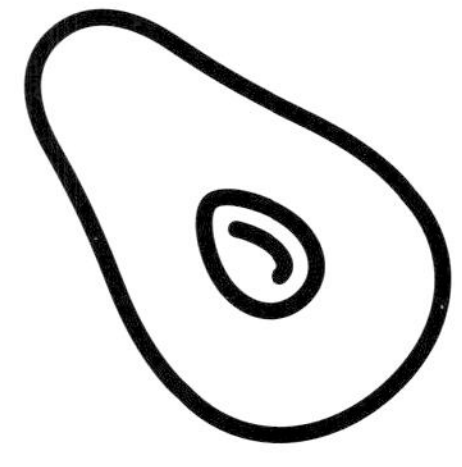

phyllo dough tacos

with ground beef, kidney beans, and guacamole

INGREDIENTS TO MAKE 12

for the guacamole

- 1 ripe avocado, mashed
- a few sprigs of cilantro, finely chopped
- 1 tomato, chopped
- ½ red onion, chopped
- ¼ tsp ground cumin
- 1 tbsp lime juice
- salt and pepper, to taste

for the tacos

- 1 green chili pepper, de-seeded and finely chopped
- 4 phyllo dough sheets
- 3½ oz ground beef
- 2 tbsp olive oil
- 1 tbsp Cajun seasoning
- ½ cup kidney beans
- ¾ cup grated cheese
- ⅜ cup sour cream

STEP 1

For the guacamole, mix together the avocado, cilantro, tomato, onion, cumin, and lime juice, then season with salt and pepper.

Cut the green chili in half, remove the seeds, and finely chop. Cut the phyllo dough sheets into six pieces. Press a piece of phyllo dough into a cupcake tin, and place another piece crosswise on top. Continue until all the phyllo is used.

STEP 2

Preheat the air fryer to 350°F. Place a bowl in the air fryer and bake the ground beef with the olive oil and Cajun seasoning for 6–7 minutes. Loosen with a fork during cooking. Add the green chili pepper in the last 2 minutes of cooking.

Reduce the air fryer temperature to 325°F. Combine the beef mixture with the kidney beans, and season with salt and pepper. Divide the beef and bean mixture between the 12 phyllo dough tacos. Distribute the grated cheese on top and bake the tacos for about 8 minutes.

STEP 3

Top the tacos with guacamole and sour cream to serve.

Serve the rest of
the guacamole
and crème fraîche
separately.

burritos
with chicken and garlic mayonnaise

INGREDIENTS TO SERVE 4

for the garlic mayonnaise

- 2 garlic cloves, crushed
- ¼ cup / 2 fl oz mayonnaise

for the burritos

- 1 lb chicken fillet, diced
- 2 tbsp olive oil
- 2 tbsp Mexican seasoning
- pinch of salt
- 1 red onion, halved and sliced
- 1 can whole kernel corn
- 1 avocado, diced
- 4 flour tortillas

STEP 1

Stir the crushed garlic into the mayonnaise and refrigerate.

Mix the chicken with the olive oil, Mexican seasoning, and a pinch of salt. Leave the chicken to marinate in the refrigerator for 30 minutes.

STEP 2

Preheat the air fryer to 350°F. Put the chicken in the air fryer basket, and cook for about 6 minutes. Shake the basket occasionally so the cubes brown nicely on all sides. Transfer the cooked chicken to a bowl, and stir in the onion and corn. Briefly return the bowl to the air fryer to warm up the filling. Then warm the tortillas for 1–2 minutes.

STEP 3

Mix the diced avocado with the warm burrito filling. Place a tortilla on a plate, spoon some of the filling on top, and roll up the tortilla. Make the other 3 tortillas the same way. Serve the garlic mayonnaise separately.

churrasco tortillas

with chimichurri sauce

INGREDIENTS TO SERVE 4

- juice of 2 limes
- 1 onion, grated
- 1½ tbsp red wine vinegar
- 1½ tbsp Worcestershire sauce
- 3 tsp chili flakes
- 1 tsp cumin seeds
- 2 tsp oregano
- 7 tbsp olive oil
- 5 garlic cloves
- 1 lb rib eye steak
- 1 handful cilantro leaves, finely chopped
- 1 handful flat-leaf parsley, finely chopped
- 3 fresh mint leaves, finely chopped
- 1 large shallot
- 1 green chili pepper
- 2 tbsp white wine vinegar
- salt and pepper, to taste
- 2 grilled bell peppers
- 4 flour tortillas

STEP 1

Mix the lime juice, onion, red wine vinegar, Worcestershire sauce, chili flakes, cumin seeds, oregano, and 2 tablespoons of olive oil until well blended. Crush 3 garlic cloves and stir into the mixture. Place the steak in the marinade and leave to marinate for at least 8 hours.

For the chimichurri, finely chop the cilantro, parsley, and mint, then mix with 5 tbsp olive oil. Finely chop 2 garlic cloves, the shallot, and chili pepper, and stir into the oil. Add the white wine vinegar and season the chimichurri to taste with salt and pepper. Cut the bell peppers into strips. Pat the steak dry.

STEP 2

Preheat the air fryer to 350°F. Warm the tortillas in the air fryer for 1–2 m nutes. Then grill the meat—preferably on a grill plate—for 2–3 m nutes on each side; it is then medium on the inside.

STEP 3

Cut the meat into strips. Top the wraps with the bell pepper and strips of steak, then season with salt and pepper. Drizzle the chimichurri sauce on top. Serve the churrasco tortillas immediately.

jalapeños

with bacon and cream cheese

INGREDIENTS TO MAKE 16

for the jalapeño peppers

- ¾ cup / 6 oz cream cheese
- 1 tsp paprika
- ½ bunch cilantro, finely chopped
- pinch of cayenne pepper
- pinch of salt
- 8 fresh green jalapeños, de-seeded and halved
- 16 bacon slices

for serving

- sprigs of fresh cilantro
- paprika

STEP 1

Mix the cream cheese with the paprika and cilantro. Season to taste with a pinch of cayenne pepper and salt. Fill the jalapeños with the cream cheese, then wrap in a bacon slice.

STEP 2

Preheat the air fryer to 350°F. Place a batch of the jalapeños in the basket and bake for 5–6 minutes until the bacon is crispy. Bake the rest of the jalapeños the same way.

STEP 3

Cut off the cilantro leaves. Place the jalapeños on a dish, and sprinkle with paprika and coriander leaves.

SERVING TIP

Serve the jalapeños with white rice, a tomato salad, and a bowl of kidney beans. Or serve them as an appetizer.

chicken meatballs
with ras el hanout and fresh herbs

INGREDIENTS TO SERVE 4

- 1¼ lb ground chicken
- 3½ oz soft goat cheese
- 1 shallot, minced
- ¼ cup finely chopped fresh herbs (e.g., chives and parsley)
- 1 tsp paprika
- 1 tsp ras el hanout
- 1 egg
- 3 tbsp breadcrumbs
- salt and pepper, to taste
- dash of chicken broth (fresh or cube)

Ras el hanout is a traditional Moroccan spice blend. It is delicious in combination with ground chicken.

STEP 1

Knead together the ground chicken, goat cheese, shallot, herbs, paprika, ras el hanout, egg, and breadcrumbs until well combined. Season with salt and pepper, then form the mixture into small meatballs.

STEP 2

Preheat the air fryer to 350°F. Remove the basket. Pour a layer of chicken broth into the air fryer and return the basket. Place (a batch of) the balls in the basket and cover with aluminum foil. Steam the balls for 20 minutes until done. Carefully remove the foil.

SERVING TIP

Serve the meatballs with pilaf, spiced rice, or couscous, or try them on a tomato and cucumber salad.

crostini

with bacon and mozzarella

INGREDIENTS TO MAKE 12–14

for the crostini

- ½ baguette, cut into ½-inch slices
- 1 garlic clove, crushed
- ½ cup / 4 fl oz olive oil
- coarsely ground pepper and sea salt, to taste

for the topping

- 6–7 pieces of bacon
- 12–14 mini mozzarella balls
- 2 green onions, chopped

Crostini are thin slices of baguette, brushed with oil and garlic, and toasted. They make the perfect base for all kinds of delicious toppings.

STEP 1

Preheat the air fryer to 350°F. Place 6–7 slices of bread in the air fryer basket. Mix the crushed garlic with the olive oil. Drizzle some of the garlic oil over the bread slices. Sprinkle coarsely ground pepper and sea salt on top. Bake the slices until golden brown and crispy, about 4 minutes. Bake the other baguette slices the same way.

STEP 2

Place the bacon slices in the air fryer basket and bake for about 4 minutes, until crispy. Drain on paper towel, then cut in half. Cut the mini mozzarella balls in half and place on the baguette slices. Top with a half slice of bacon and a sprinkling of green onions

sesame pastry
with savory chicken filling

INGREDIENTS TO MAKE 8

for the filling

- 6 cups / 48 fl oz chicken broth
- 7 oz chicken fillet
- 1 red chili pepper, de-seeded and finely chopped
- 1 bunch cilantro, finely chopped
- 3 garlic cloves, finely chopped
- 1½ cups fresh peas
- ¼ cup / 2 fl oz soy sauce

for the dough

- 4 cups glutinous rice flour
- 1 cup powdered sugar
- 1⅔ cup / 13½ fl oz coconut milk
- pinch coarse sea salt
- ⅔ cup sesame seeds

STEP 1

Bring the chicken broth to a boil on the stove top. Add the chicken fillet and cook until done, about 20 minutes. Remove the chicken from the broth and shred the fillet using two forks. Put the pieces of chicken, red chili pepper, cilantro, garlic, peas, and soy sauce in a bowl. Mix until well combined.

STEP 2

Mix the rice flour, powdered sugar, coconut milk, and a pinch of sea salt to a solid dough. Form it into balls about the size of a ping-pong ball. Flatten each dough ball in your hand and spoon some of the filling on top. Close the dough and pinch it firmly to join it, then form back into a ball. Roll the ball over the sesame seeds until coated.

STEP 3

Preheat the air fryer to 350°F. Place half of the balls in the air fryer basket and bake for 5–6 minutes until golden brown. Bake the other half the same way.

Delicious
with rice
and a fresh
cucumber
salad.

Delicious
with fresh
mashed potatoes
or nut rice and
a crispy salad.

stuffed tomatoes
with ground beef

INGREDIENTS TO SERVE 4

- 3 tbsp mild olive oil
- 2 garlic cloves, crushed
- 3½ oz ground beef
- 8 beefsteak tomatoes
- 2 oz grated parmesan cheese
- ½ red pepper, de-seeded and finely chopped
- 2 tbsp parsley, finely chopped, plus extra for garnish
- ½ cup fine breadcrumbs
- ½ cup / 4 oz butter
- salt and pepper, to taste

STEP 1

Heat 1 tablespoon of olive oil and fry the garlic and ground beef on the stove top until browned.

STEP 2

Preheat the air fryer to 400°F. Cut off the cap of the tomatoes and hollow them out. Spoon the cheese, red pepper, and parsley into the mince mixture and season with salt and pepper. Stuff the tomatoes with the mixture. Place a batch of the tomatoes in the air fryer basket. Distribute a tablespoon of breadcrumbs and a half tablespoon of butter over each tomato, then bake for 8–10 minutes.

STEP 3

Place 2 tomatoes on each plate and garnish with parsley.

chicken tenders
in cola-whiskey marinade

INGREDIENTS TO SERVE 4

for the marinade

- ½ cup / 4 fl oz cola
- 2 tbsp barbecue sauce
- 2 tbsp whiskey
- 2 tbsp honey
- 4 garlic cloves, crushed
- coarsely ground pepper and sea salt, to taste

for the chicken

- 1 lb chicken tenders, cut into pieces

for serving

- 2 limes, cut into wedges
- ½ cup / 4 fl oz barbecue sauce
- 4 sprigs of watercress

STEP 1

Combine the cola, barbecue sauce, whiskey, and honey in a mixing bowl. Stir the garlic into the marinade. Season to taste with coarsely ground pepper and sea salt. Add the chicken to the marinade, and mix well to coat all the chicken. Leave the chicken to marinate in the fridge for 3 hours.

STEP 2

Remove the chicken and pour the marinade into a saucepan. Let the marinade reduce on the stove top over medium heat for 10–15 minutes. Preheat the air fryer to 350°F. Place the chicken in the basket lined with parchment paper, and bake for 8–10 minutes, shaking the basket occasionally, until golden brown on all sides.

STEP 3

Stir the reduced marinade into the barbecue sauce. Serve the chicken with the sauce, lime wedges, and sprigs of watercress.

SERVING TIP

Serve with a fresh watercress salad and warm pita breads.

Drink with
India Pale Ale
(IPA).

roast beef
with herbed potatoes

INGREDIENTS TO SERVE 4

- 1¼ lb roast beef
- salt and pepper, to taste
- 1½ lb small potatoes, cut into small pieces
- ¾ cup cherry tomatoes (about 20–25)
- ¼ cup / 2 fl oz olive oil
- 2 sprigs of thyme, finely chopped
- 2 sprigs of rosemary, finely chopped
- 2 garlic cloves, finely chopped

The potatoes and tomatoes turn this dish into a complete meal, but if you like, you can serve it with a fresh salad.

STEP 1

Preheat the air fryer to 400°F. Place the roast beef in the basket. Sprinkle the meat with salt and pepper, then bake for 10 minutes. Lower the temperature to 350°F and bake for another 20 minutes. Check the internal temperature with a meat thermometer: at 130°F the meat is medium-rare. Remove the meat from the air fryer and leave to rest covered with aluminum foil.

STEP 2

Pat the potatoes dry and combine with the olive oil, thyme, rosemary, and cloves. Season to taste with salt and pepper. Distribute the potatoes in the air fryer basket and cook for about 15 minutes at 350°F, shaking the basket occasionally. Add the cherry tomatoes 3 minutes before the end of the cooking time.

STEP 3

Cut the roast beef into slices and divide the meat between the plates. Serve with the potatoes and tomatoes.

Brazilian croquettes

with spicy marinated chicken

INGREDIENTS TO MAKE 16

- 2 chicken fillets
- 1 shallot, finely chopped
- 2 garlic cloves, finely chopped
- 1 carrot, peeled and diced
- 1 bay leaf
- chicken broth from a cube
- ¾ cup / 6 oz cream cheese
- 4 green onions, chopped
- ½ green pepper, finely chopped
- ½ red pepper, finely chopped
- salt and pepper, to taste
- 1 cup flour
- 2 eggs
- ⅔ cup breadcrumbs

STEP 1

On the stove top, gently bring the chicken fillets with the shallot, garlic, carrot, and bay leaf to a boil in the broth. Allow the chicken to cook for 10–15 minutes. Remove the chicken fillet and strain the broth. Keep 1½ cup / 12 fl oz broth aside. Cut or shred the chicken fillets into small pieces. Mix the chicken chunks with the cream cheese, green onions, and peppers, then season with salt and pepper. Chill the chicken mixture for at least 30 minutes. Bring the measured amount of broth back to a boil and gradually stir in the sifted flour. After a few minutes, a firm dough will be formed. Place in a bowl to cool, then refrigerate until the dough is firm enough to roll out.

Divide the dough into 16 portions and roll into balls.

STEP 2

Divide the chicken mixture into 16 portions. Flatten the dough balls by pressing or rolling, and place a portion of chicken on top. Fold the dough over the chicken and form into a pear shape. Sprinkle the "pears" with flour. Beat the eggs. Roll the "pears" through the egg mixture, then through the breadcrumbs. Place on a sheet of parchment paper in the fridge and leave to chill for at least 1 hour. Preheat the air fryer to 400°F. Bake the Brazilian croquettes in the air fryer in batches of 4, about 13 minutes.

Drink with
India Pale Ale
(IPA).

spicy marinated

chicken wings

INGREDIENTS TO SERVE 4

- 2 tbsp hoisin sauce
- 5 tbsp honey
- 1-inch ginger root, peeled and grated
- 1 garlic clove, crushed
- 5 green onions
- 1 lb chicken wings
- 1 red chili pepper, sliced
- 4 sprigs of cilantro
- ¼ cup / 2 fl oz barbecue sauce
- ¼ cup / 2 fl oz lime oil*

* LIME OIL

Put the peel of two limes in a 16 fl oz bottle of olive oil and leave overnight.

Start preparing this delicious appetizer one day in advance, as it takes time to make the marinade and lime oil.

STEP 1

Mix together the hoisin sauce, honey, ginger, garlic. Very thinly slice the green onions or grind into a paste in the food processor. Add the green onions to the marinade. Place the chicken wings in the marinade and mix until well coated. Cover the bowl and refrigerate for at least 8 hours. This will allow the marinade to penetrate and tenderize the meat and enrich its flavor.

STEP 2

Preheat the air fryer to 400°F. Place a batch of the chicken wings in the air fryer basket and bake for 10 minutes. Lower the temperature to 325°F and bake the wings for an additional 10 minutes.

STEP 3

Sprinkle the red pepper and cilantro leaves over the chicken wings. Serve with barbecue sauce and lime oil as a dip.

good vibes

Vegetarian

Serving tip: bake a piece of salmon and serve it with the spinach tarts!

spinach tarts

INGREDIENTS TO MAKE 12

for the dough

- 2½ cups flour
- ⅔ cup / 5¼ oz butter
- pinch of salt
- 1 egg
- 2–3 tbsp cold water

for the filling

- 2 tbsp / 1 oz butter
- 1 onion, finely chopped
- 3 cups spinach, finely chopped
- 2 tbsp parsley, finely chopped
- 2 tbsp dill, finely chopped
- ½ cup / 4 fl oz heavy cream
- 2 large eggs
- 6 oz feta cheese, crumbled
- salt and pepper, to taste

STEP 1

Mix the flour, butter, salt, egg, and water to a dough. Cover in plastic wrap and leave to rest in the fridge for 30 minutes.

In a large pan, heat the butter and fry the onion for 2–3 minutes. Add the spinach and stir-fry until reduced. Stir in the parsley and dill. In another bowl, beat together heavy cream and eggs. Add the feta cheese into the egg mixture. Combine the spinach and egg mixtures, then season with salt and pepper.

Unwrap the dough, and divide it into 12 equal portions. Grease 12 cupcake molds that fit in the air fryer, and line the bottom and sides with dough. Prick holes in the bottom with a fork. Distribute the filling over the dough.

STEP 2

Preheat the air fryer to 350°F. Place 4 spinach tarts in the air fryer and bake for 10-12 minutes. Bake the rest of the spinach tarts the same way.

omelet
with turmeric and mushrooms

INGREDIENTS TO MAKE
1 LARGE OMELET

- 1 cup / 3½ oz mushrooms, sliced
- 1 small onion, sliced
- 2 tbsp olive oil
- 2 eggs
- 1 tsp turmeric
- freshly ground salt and pepper, to taste
- arugula leaves, to garnish

Craving a hearty omelet? The air fryer is at your service! This delicious breakfast or lunch is quick, easy, and healthy. Plus, with the air fryer, you don't need to worry that your omelet will burn on the bottom.

STEP 1

Remove the basket from the air fryer and preheat to 350°F. Place the mushrooms and onion in a bowl and pour the olive oil on top. Distribute the mushrooms and onions over a round baking pan or oven dish that fits into the air fryer. Bake the mushroom mixture in the air fryer for about 6 minutes.

STEP 2

Beat the eggs with the turmeric and a little salt and pepper. Use oven gloves to remove the baking pan or oven dish from the air fryer. Pour the eggs over the mushroom mixture, then return the pan or dish to the air fryer. Cook for another 5 minutes or until the surface is dry. Garnish with a few arugula leaves.

eggplant rolls

with tomatoes and goat cheese

INGREDIENTS TO MAKE 8

for the dried tomatoes / the eggplant rolls

- 16 oz cherry tomatoes (about 15–20), halved
- 3 garlic cloves
- ¾ cup / 6 fl oz extra-virgin olive oil
- ½ tbsp Italian seasoning
- 1 eggplant, cut into 8 thin slices
- 1 x 8 oz roll soft goat cheese, cut into 8 slices
- 8 sprigs of rosemary
- coarsely ground pepper and sea salt, to taste

STEP 1

Preheat the air fryer to 200°F. Coarsely chop 2 garlic cloves. Place the tomatoes and chopped garlic in the air fryer basket. Mix 4 tablespoons of olive oil with the Italian seasoning, and drizzle over the tomatoes. Sprinkle with salt and pepper. Dry the tomatoes in the air fryer for 2–2½ hours.

Increase the temperature of the air fryer to 400°F. Crush the remaining garlic clove over a bowl. Add salt, pepper, and ½ cup / 4 oz olive oil. Coat both sides of the eggplant slices with the garlic oil. Place the eggplant slices in the air fryer basket; they may slightly overlap. Bake the eggplant for 6–8 minutes.

STEP 2

Place a slice of goat cheese on each eggplant slice and top with a dried tomato and sprig of rosemary. Roll up the slices and drizzle with the remaining olive oil.

omelet
with green vegetables

INGREDIENTS TO SERVE 4

- ½ cup broccoli
- ½ cup peas
- ¼ cup fresh spinach
- 6 eggs
- salt and pepper, to taste
- 2 sprigs of flat-leaf parsley, finely chopped
- 2 tbsp heavy cream
- ½ tsp nutmeg

STEP 1

Cut the broccoli into florets, cook in lightly salted water for 3–4 minutes, then drain. Combine the broccoli florets, peas, and spinach. Beat the eggs, and season with salt and pepper. Stir most of the parsley with the cream and nutmeg into the eggs. Spoon in the vegetables.

STEP 2

Preheat the air fryer to 350°F. Grease a round oven dish that fits into the air fryer. Pour in half of the egg mixture and bake the omelet in the air fryer for 10 minutes. Remove the omelet from the oven dish, and cover with aluminum foil to keep warm. Make the second omelet the same way.

STEP 3

Cut the omelets in half and place one half on each plate. Sprinkle with the remaining parsley.

SERVING TIP

Serve with a fresh spinach salad and toasted country-style bread.

Serve the mushrooms with a spoonful of chili sauce and lemon slices.

mushrooms
in Asian-style marinade

INGREDIENTS
FOR 12–15 SATAYS

- 1 inch fresh ginger root, grated
- 1 red chili pepper, finely chopped
- 2 garlic cloves, finely chopped
- 1 shallot, finely chopped
- 1 tbsp curry powder
- 2 tbsp sweet soy sauce
- 2 tbsp parsley
- salt and pepper, to taste
- 2 portobello mushrooms
- 2 cups mushrooms

STEP 1

Make a nearly dry marinade of the ginger, red chili pepper, garlic, and shallot, combined with the curry powder, sweet soy sauce, parsley, and salt and pepper. Make sure the mixture is not too wet to prevent the mushrooms from getting soggy. Cut the portobello mushrooms into 1-inch thick cubes and cut the larger mushrooms in half. Add the mushrooms into the marinade and leave to marinate for at least 3 hours. Soak the skewers in water for at least 30 minutes.

STEP 2

Preheat the air fryer to 350°F. Thread the mushrooms onto the skewers, and place a batch of the satays in the air fryer basket. Bake 6–8 minutes, turning twice during cooking. Bake the other satays the same way.

SERVING TIP

Serve with boiled rice and a fresh salad of finely chopped Chinese cabbage mixed with cashews. Make a dressing of sesame oil, soy sauce, red wine vinegar, honey mustard, and a little bit of wasabi paste to taste.

sauerkraut rolls
with cottage cheese sauce

INGREDIENTS FOR 8 ROLLS

for the cottage cheese sauce

- 7 tbsp / 3½ oz cottage cheese
- 3½ tbsp / 2 oz crème fraîche
- 1 tbsp parsley
- ½ tsp nutmeg
- 2 hard-boiled eggs

for the sauerkraut rolls

- 8 phyllo dough sheets
- 1 x 10.6 oz can sauerkraut
- 4 dried apricots, sliced
- 4 dried prunes, sliced
- 1 tsp ground cinnamon
- 2 tbsp capers
- salt and pepper, to taste
- 5 tbsp olive oil

STEP 1

Mix together the cottage cheese, crème fraîche, parsley, and nutmeg. Season to taste with salt and pepper. Cut the eggs in half, transfer to a bowl, and spoon the cottage cheese mixture on top.

Thaw the phyllo dough sheets. Rinse the sauerkraut with hot water, drain, and squeeze out moisture. Mix the dried apricots and prunes, ground cinnamon, and capers into the sauerkraut. Season to taste with salt and pepper. Rub the phyllo dough sheets with olive oil and place a spoonful of sauerkraut mixture at the bottom corner of each sheet. Fold in the sides and firmly roll up the rest. Brush with olive oil on the outside.

STEP 2

Preheat the air fryer to 350°F. Place the sauerkraut rolls in the air fryer and cook until golden brown and crispy, about 7–8 minutes.

STEP 3

Serve with the cottage cheese sauce.

Serving tip: serve the rolls with creamy mashed pumpkin (see page 19) or sweet potatoes.

spring rolls
with vegetables and tempeh

INGREDIENTS TO MAKE 8

for the spring rolls

- 7 oz rice noodles
- 1¼ cup / 7 oz tempeh
- 1 red or green chili pepper, de-seeded and sliced
- 1 leek, sliced
- ½ Chinese cabbage, sliced
- 4 garlic cloves, minced
- olive oil, for stir-frying
- 1 tsp ground cumin
- ½ cup soybeans
- 8 spring roll sheets

for serving

- 2 tbsp nigella seeds
- ½ cup / 4 fl oz chili sauce

STEP 1

Cook the rice noodles, according to the package instructions, until tender.

STEP 2

Preheat the air fryer to 350°F. Crumble the tempeh, put in an oven dish that fits in the air fryer, and cook for 5 minutes. Transfer the tempeh to a bowl and set aside.

Stir-fry the leeks, pepper, garlic, and cabbage in a little olive oil until the leeks are completely soft. Add the cumin and soybeans. Cook the vegetables for 5 minutes, then add the tempeh and rice noodles.

Place a spring roll sheet on the work surface and spoon the filling onto the center of the sheet. Fold in the sides. Roll up the spring roll and secure the tip with water. Make the other spring rolls the same way. Place 4 spring rolls in the air fryer basket and cook for 8–10 minutes, until golden brown and crispy. Cook the other 4 spring rolls the same way.

STEP 3

Sprinkle the nigella seeds over the spring rolls and serve with a bowl of chili sauce.

ratatouille

INGREDIENTS TO SERVE 4

- ½ green zucchini, sliced
- ½ yellow zucchini, sliced
- 1 small eggplant, sliced
- 1 red onion, sliced
- 1 beefsteak tomato, sliced
- 4 sprigs of thyme
- olive oil
- salt and pepper, to taste

STEP 1

Arrange the slices of zucchini, eggplant, onion, and tomato, alternating and slightly overlapping, in two oven dishes that fit into the air fryer. Drizzle generously with olive oil and sprinkle with the thyme leaves and a little salt and pepper.

STEP 2

Preheat the air fryer to 350°F. Place one oven dish in the air fryer and cook the ratatouille for 15–20 minutes. Cook the second batch the same way.

SERVING TIP

Serve the ratatouille with pasta and a piece of roasted fish or steak.

A colorful dish full of vegetables!

A vegetarian tofu dish with a delicious herb mix.

tofu teriyaki
with white rice

INGREDIENTS TO SERVE 4

- 3 garlic cloves, minced
- ¼ cup / 2 fl oz soy sauce
- 2 tbsp / 1 fl oz spicy chili sauce
- 2 tbsp sugar
- 2 tbsp smooth peanut butter
- 2 tbsp / 1 fl oz sesame oil
- 1 tbsp sesame seeds
- 1 block of organic tofu (about 14 oz), cubed
- 3½ oz snap peas (about 7), cut into thin strips or diamonds
- 2 tbsp olive oil
- 1¼ cup / 5 oz white rice
- 1 red chili pepper, sliced
- 4 sprigs of cilantro, coarsely chopped

STEP 1

Combine the garlic, soy sauce, chili sauce, sugar, peanut butter, sesame oil, and sesame seeds to make a marinade. Heat the olive oil in a sauce pan, and fry the tofu cubes until they begin to color, stirring constantly. Spoon in the beans, add the marinade, then refrigerate for 30 minutes.

Cook the rice according to the package instructions, until tender, and keep warm.

STEP 2

Preheat the air fryer to 400°F. Put the tofu-bean mixture with the marinade in an oven dish that fits into the air fryer. Cook for 5–7 minutes, stirring occasionally.

STEP 3

Distribute the rice over the plates, and spoon the tofu teriyaki on top. Garnish with chili pepper and cilantro.

SERVING TIP

This dish is delicious served with fresh cucumber slices.

risotto cakes

with mascarpone dip

INGREDIENTS TO MAKE 8

for the risotto cakes

- 2 cups mixed mushrooms, finely chopped
- 1 onion, finely chopped
- 2 garlic cloves, finely chopped
- dash of extra-virgin olive oil
- 1¼ cup risotto rice
- 1 tsp dried thyme
- 2 cups / 16 fl oz mushroom broth
- ⅔ cup / 5¼ fl oz white wine
- ½ cup / 3½ oz gorgonzola
- 1 cup breadcrumbs

for the mascarpone dip

- ½ cup / 3½ oz mascarpone
- 1 tbsp dill

STEP 1

Fry the mushrooms, onion, and garlic in a dash of olive oil. When the onion is softened, add the risotto rice and thyme, and cook for another minute. Gradually add the mushroom broth and white wine, until the rice has absorbed all the moisture. Stir the risotto occasionally. Add some extra broth if the rice is not completely tender. Stir the gorgonzola into the risotto and allow to cool. Roll the risotto into balls about the size of a ping-pong ball, then flatten lightly. Sprinkle the breadcrumbs onto a plate, and coat the cakes in the breadcrumbs.

STEP 2

Preheat the air fryer to 400°F. Place half of the cakes in the air fryer basket and cook until golden brown, about 15 minutes. Cook the other half the same way.

STEP 3

Mix the mascarpone and dill to make a dipping sauce. Serve the cakes with the mascarpone dip.

SERVING TIP

Serve with a fresh tomato salad of cherry tomatoes and arugula with a dressing of olive oil, balsamic vinegar, thyme, and salt and pepper.

This is how you get those 7 ounces of vegetables per day!

roasted vegetables

in the Italian style

INGREDIENTS TO SERVE 4

- 3½ oz broccolini
- 7 oz green beans
- 7 oz cherry tomatoes
- 2 red onions
- 1 eggplant
- 1 zucchini
- 1 cup gorgonzola
- 2 tbsp olive oil
- 4 sprigs of basil

STEP 1

Clean the broccolini and green beans. Cut the cherry tomatoes in half and slice the onion into half rings. Cut the eggplant and zucchini into cubes. Crumble the gorgonzola.

STEP 2

Preheat the air fryer to 400°F. Mix all vegetables with the olive oil in a bowl, then transfer the vegetables to the air fryer basket. Lower the temperature to 325°F. Cook the vegetables for 10–12 minutes, shaking the basket occasionally.

Return the vegetables to the bowl, sprinkle the gorgonzola on top, then return the bowl to the air fryer for 2–3 minutes to allow the cheese to slightly melt.

SERVING TIP

Delicious with boiled pasta or rice. This dish can also be served with half of the ratatouille (see page 44) and chicken souvlaki (see page 59).

pumpkin mash
with chickpeas and mint

INGREDIENTS TO SERVE 4

for the labneh

- 4¼ cups / 34 fl oz full-fat yogurt
- ½ tbsp za'atar seasoning
- 1 tsp salt
- drizzle of olive oil

for the pumpkin mash

- ¼ cup / 2 fl oz extra-virgin olive oil
- ½ cup / 4 fl oz labneh
- 1 tsp cumin seeds
- coarsely ground pepper and sea salt, to taste
- 2 garlic cloves, crushed
- 7 oz cooking pumpkin, peeled and cut into thin slices
- 4 sprigs of cilantro, finely chopped
- 1 x 7 oz can chickpeas
- 1 green onion, sliced
- 1 tbsp sesame seeds
- fresh mint

STEP 1

For the labneh, place a towel-lined strainer over a bowl and pour in the yogurt. Strain the yogurt overnight. Mix the strained yogurt with the za'atar seasoning and salt. Drizzle some olive oil on top.

Mix the olive oil with the labneh, cumin seeds, and coarsely ground pepper and sea salt. Add the garlic to the oil-yogurt mixture and stir until well blended.

STEP 2

Preheat the air fryer to 350°F. Place the pumpkin slices in the air fryer and roast for 12–15 minutes, until tender.

STEP 3

Coarsely mash the pumpkin and stir in the oil-yogurt mixture. Add the cilantro leaves and chickpeas, stirring until well combined. Sprinkle the green onion over the pumpkin mash. Sprinkle the sesame seeds on top and garnish with fresh mint leaves.

SERVING TIP

Spicy meatballs (see page 70) and a bowl of hummus combine well with this pumpkin mash.

roasted cauliflower

with cumin-yogurt sauce

INGREDIENTS TO SERVE 2-4

for the cauliflower

- 2 tbsp olive oil
- 1 tsp turmeric
- ½ tsp ground cumin
- 1 tsp cilantro seeds
- pepper and sea salt, to taste
- 1 small cauliflower, cut into florets

for the yogurt sauce

- ⅔ cup / 5¼ fl oz Greek yogurt
- 1 tbsp mayonnaise
- ½ tsp ground cumin
- salt and pepper, to taste

for serving

- 1 tbsp flat-leaf parsley
- 1 tbsp dill

STEP 1

Mix together the olive oil, turmeric, cumin, and cilantro seeds, then season with salt and pepper. Coat the cauliflower florets with the spice mixture until fully covered. Let the cauliflower to marinate for 30 minutes.

To make the yogurt sauce, beat together the yogurt, mayonnaise, and cumin, then season with salt and pepper.

STEP 2

Preheat the air fryer to 400°F. Distribute the cauliflower florets over the air fryer basket. Roast the cauliflower for 8–10 minutes, shaking the basket occasionally, until browned and tender.

STEP 3

Transfer the cauliflower to a bowl, sprinkle with parsley and dill, and serve with the yogurt sauce.

falafel
with hummus and labneh

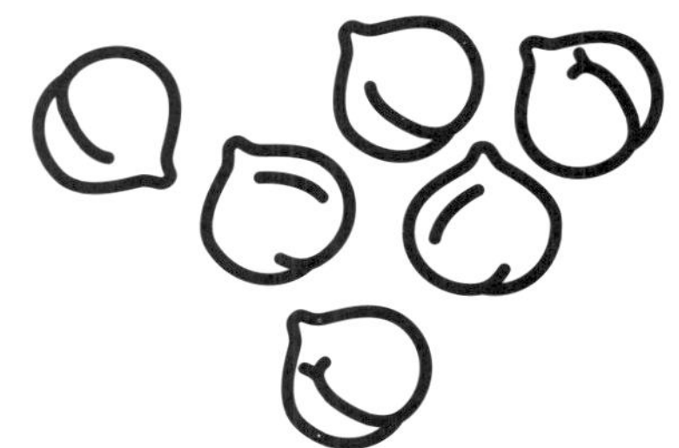

INGREDIENTS TO SERVE 4

- 2 x 14 oz can precooked chickpeas
- 2 garlic cloves
- 1 tsp dried parsley
- 2 tsp dried cilantro
- ¼ tsp cayenne pepper
- ½ tsp ground cumin
- 3 tbsp flour
- 2 pinches of salt
- 3½ oz tahini
- 2 tbsp lemon juice
- ⅓–½ cup / 2½-4 fl oz ice water
- flat-leaf parsley
- 1 lemon
- 4½ cups labneh (see page 136)

STEP 1

For the falafel, finely grind 1¼ cans / 17½ oz chickpeas with 1 garlic clove in the food processor. Add the parsley, cilantro, cayenne pepper, cumin, flour, and a pinch of salt. Mix until well combined, cover the dough, and refrigerate for 1 hour. Shape into small balls and flatten.

For the hummus, grind the remaining chickpeas with 1 garlic clove in the food processor to a solid puree. Add the tahini, lemon juice, and a pinch of salt while grinding. Pour in the ice water in a thin stream, stirring until a smooth and creamy puree is formed.

STEP 2

Preheat the air fryer to 350°F. Bake the falafel in batches in the air fryer basket until golden brown, about 8–10 minutes. Shake the basket occasionally to ensure the falafel are browned on all sides.

STEP 3

Place the falafel on a serving plate and sprinkle with parsley. Cut the lemon into wedges and add to the dish. Serve with hummus and labneh.

Serving tip: sprinkle the labneh to taste with black olive rings.

halloumi sticks

with pomegranate and mint yogurt

INGREDIENTS

FOR 2 BOWLS

for the halloumi

- 3 tbsp olive oil
- 1 garlic clove, crushed
- salt and pepper, to taste
- 1 lb halloumi, cut into sticks

for the mint-yogurt sauce

- $^{2}/_{3}$ cup / 5¼ fl oz thick yogurt
- 1 tbsp sour cream
- 2 tbsp mint
- salt and pepper, to taste

for serving

- ¼ cup pomegranate arils

STEP 1

Combine the olive oil and crushed garlic in a bowl. Add salt and pepper, then stir in the garlic oil until well combined. Coat the halloumi slices with the garlic oil.

Make a mint-yogurt sauce by beating together the yogurt, sour cream, mint, and salt and pepper.

STEP 2

Preheat the air fryer to 400°F. Distribute the halloumi in portions over the air fryer basket, and bake until golden brown, about 20 minutes.

STEP 3

Divide the halloumi between the plates, drizzle the mint-yogurt sauce on top, and garnish with the pomegranate arils.

SERVING TIP

For a complete meal, serve the halloumi with a bowl of bulgur and roasted cauliflower (see page 139).

mini wraps

with roasted sweet potatoes and salad

INGREDIENTS TO MAKE 4

- 2 large sweet potatoes, cut into wedges
- 4 sprigs of rosemary
- 1 tsp sea salt
- 5 tbsp extra-virgin olive oil
- zest and juice of 1 lemon
- ¼ cup / 2 fl oz extra-virgin olive oil
- 1 garlic clove, crushed
- coarsely ground pepper and sea salt, to taste
- 1 cup red cabbage, finely chopped
- ¼ cup chard
- ¼ cup watercress
- 4 small flour wraps or tortillas
- ¾ cup pomegranate arils
- fresh parsley, to garnish

STEP 1

Preheat the air fryer to 350°F. Place the sweet potato wedges in the air fryer basket. Strip off the rosemary leaves and sprinkle with the salt over the potatoes.

Drizzle the potato wedges with olive oil, toss, and roast until golden brown, about 15 minutes. Toss occasionally during cooking.

STEP 2

Mix the lemon juice and zest and olive oil in a bowl. Stir in the crushed garlic. Season with salt and pepper.

STEP 3

Distribute the red cabbage, chard, and watercress across the wraps. Remove the sweet potato wedges from the air fryer, and arrange them over the vegetables. Drizzle with the dressing and top with pomegranate arils. Garnish with fresh parsley.

pizza

with tomatoes and olives

INGREDIENTS FOR
4 SMALL PIZZAS

- 4 cups all-purpose flour
- ½ tsp salt
- 1 tsp dry active yeast
- ½ tbsp sugar
- ¼ cup / 2 fl oz olive oil
- 1 cup / 8 fl oz lukewarm water
- ½ cup / 4 fl oz spicy tomato sauce
- 1 cup / 5 oz cherry tomatoes, cut in half
- ½ cup / 3½ oz kalamata and green olives
- fresh rosemary and thyme

STEP 1

Put the flour in a bowl, and add the salt. Make a well in the middle. Mix together the yeast, sugar, olive oil, and water, then leave the mixture to rest for a few minutes. Pour the mixture into the well and start combining from the outside in. Knead the dough to a smooth, even consistency. Cover the bowl with a moist kitchen towel and leave the dough to rise for 60 minutes. Divide the dough into 4 equal portions, and roll out each portion into a round pizza base that fits into the air fryer.

STEP 2

Preheat the air fryer to 350°F. Spread the pizzas with tomato sauce and top with vine tomatoes and olives. Sprinkle with fresh rosemary and thyme. Bake the pizzas one by one in the basket until golden brown, about 8–10 minutes per pizza.

VARIATION TIP

Do you like meat or fish? Top the pizzas with chicken strips, salami, smoked salmon, or canned tuna.

potato wedges
with lemon mayonnaise

INGREDIENTS TO SERVE 4

for the lemon mayonnaise

- 1½ cups / 12 fl oz mayonnaise
- zest of 1 lemon
- 1 tsp fresh dill
- 1 garlic clove, crushed

for the potatoes

- ¼ cup / 2 fl oz olive oil
- 1 garlic clove, crushed
- a few sprigs of rosemary
- 12 large russet potatoes, peeled and cut into wedges
- coarsely ground salt and pepper, to taste

STEP 1

Mix the mayonnaise with the lemon zest, dill, and garlic.

STEP 2

Preheat the air fryer to 300°F. Combine the olive oil and garlic, then spoon the garlic oil and rosemary over the potato wedges. Sprinkle the potato wedges with salt and pepper, transfer to the air fryer basket, and roast for 10 minutes, shaking occasionally. Increase the temperature to 350°F after 10 minutes and bake for another 10–15 minutes, until they are golden brown.

STEP 3

Sprinkle fresh rosemary and sea salt over the potatoes, and serve with the lemon mayonnaise.

vegetarian quiche
with leeks

INGREDIENTS FOR 1 LARGE OR 2 SMALL QUICHES

for the dough

- 1 tsp dry active yeast
- 1 tsp sugar
- ½ cup / 4 fl oz lukewarm milk
- 2 cups wheat flour
- 1 egg
- 7 tbsp / 3½ oz butter
- 1 tsp salt

for the filling

- 3 eggs
- 1¼ cup / 10 fl oz cream
- salt and pepper, to taste
- 1 cup mushrooms, thinly sliced
- ½ cup onion, finely chopped
- 1 large potato, diced
- 1 large leek, thinly sliced
- 2½ cups / 10½ oz grated cheddar cheese

STEP 1

Put the yeast and sugar in a bowl, and combine with the milk. Let the yeast mixture rest for a few minutes. Sift the flour over a large bowl, and make a well in the middle. Add the egg, butter, salt, and yeast mixture. Knead the dough from the inside out to form a perfect dough ball. Cover the bowl with a kitchen towel and let the dough rise for 1 hour.

To make the filling, beat together eggs, cream, and a little salt and pepper. Refrigerate the egg mixture.

STEP 2

Remove the dough from the bowl, and divide it into 2 equal portions. Grease a springform pan that fits into the air fryer. Roll out the dough between 2 sheets of parchment paper so that it covers the bottom and edges of the pan. Firmly press the dough into the pan, and prick holes in the bottom with a fork. Fill with half of the mushrooms, the onion, potato, leeks, and cheese. Season to taste with salt and pepper. Pour in half of the egg mixture and fold the overhanging dough inside.

STEP 3

Preheat the air fryer to 325°F, and bake the quiches for 30 minutes each.

grilled zucchini
with balsamic dressing

INGREDIENTS TO SERVE 4

for the zucchini

- 2 large zucchinis, sliced about ¼-inch thick
- 1 garlic clove, minced
- juice of 1 lemon
- ¼ cup / 2 fl oz olive oil
- salt and pepper, to taste

for the dressing

- ¼ cup / 2 fl oz olive oil
- 2 tbsp balsamic vinegar
- 1 tsp mustard
- 2 sun-dried tomatoes, finely chopped
- salt and pepper, to taste

Vegetables naturally contain large quantities of water, which makes them perfect for cooking in the air fryer. Use fresh-cut rather than precut bagged vegetables. Vegetables like Chioggia beet, beet, sugar snaps, bell peppers, zucchini, onions, cherry tomatoes, celery, and eggplant are perfect for cooking in the air fryer. Cut the vegetables into equal pieces to ensure even cooking. Rinse the vegetables, drain, and put in the air fryer. Grill the vegetables at 400°F, about 6–7 minutes.

STEP 1

Mix together the olive oil, garlic, lemon juice, and a little salt and pepper. Coat the zucchini slices in the oil mixture.

STEP 2

Preheat the air fryer to 400°F. Place a few zucchini slices in the air fryer basket. They may overlap slightly. Bake the zucchini in batches for 6–7 minutes. Keep the air-fried slices warm. Using a hand mixer, beat together the olive oil, balsamic vinegar, and mustard. Stir the sun-dried tomatoes into the dressing. Season with salt and pepper.

STEP 3

Place the grilled zucchini on a plate and drizzle with the dressing to serve.

Delicious with feta crumble and toasted pine nuts!

carrot fries

with za'atar dip and carrot chutney

INGREDIENTS FOR 2 SERVINGS

for the za'atar dip

- 1 tbsp mayonnaise
- 1 tbsp Greek yogurt
- 1 tbsp za'atar seasoning
- salt and pepper, to taste

for the carrot chutney

- 2 large carrots, cut into strips
- 1 small red chili pepper, de-seeded and finely chopped
- 1 shallot, minced
- 2 sprigs of thyme
- 2 tbsp olive oil
- ½ cup sugar
- ¾ cup / 6 fl oz vinegar
- 1 tsp mustard seed

for the carrot fries

- 4 large carrots
- 1 tbsp olive oil
- 1 tsp paprika
- 1 tsp dried thyme

STEP 1

First make the dip and chutney. Beat together the mayonnaise, yogurt, and za'atar, then season with salt and pepper.

Heat the olive oil and sauté the carrots, red pepper, and shallot on the stove top over medium heat for 5–8 minutes. Then add the sugar, vinegar, mustard seed, and thyme. Leave to simmer gently for 15 minutes, uncovered, stirring occasionally. Season with salt and pepper. Transfer the chutney to a bowl and allow to cool.

STEP 2

Peel the carrots for the fries and cut lengthwise into thin strips. In a bowl, combine the olive oil, paprika, thyme, and salt and pepper. Spoon in the carrot fries. Preheat the air fryer to 400°F. Place the fries in the basket and fry for 6 minutes, tossing halfway through cooking.

STEP 3

Serve the carrot fries with the za'atar dip and carrot chutney. Sprinkle with fresh thyme to taste.

vegetable chips

INGREDIENTS TO SERVE 4

- 1 large carrot, peeled and very thinly sliced
- ½ celery root, peeled, quartered and very thinly sliced
- 1 parsnip, very thinly sliced
- 1 large sweet potato, very thinly sliced
- 1 beet, very thinly sliced
- 1 apple, very thinly sliced
- cooking spray oil
- salt and pepper, to taste

For this recipe, you will need to slice the vegetables very thinly. For the best results, use a mandoline or other slicing tool that can create thin, regular slices.

STEP 1

Peel the carrot and celery root. Scrub the skin of the parsnip, potato, beet, and apple. Remove the core of the apple with an apple corer. Cut the vegetables, potato, and apple into very thin slices using a mandoline, thin slicer, or kitchen appliance that will create fine slices.

STEP 2

Preheat the air fryer to 275°F. Bake the chips in small batches until dry, 8–10 minutes per batch. Increase the temperature to 350°F. Spray the chips with oil, and sprinkle with salt and pepper.

Fry the chips, again in batches, for an additional 10 minutes, tossing occasionally. Place the chips on parchment paper, and distribute evenly to help them crisp up.

spicy tempeh

INGREDIENTS TO SERVE 4

- 1 red chili pepper, de-seeded and finely chopped
- 2 garlic cloves, finely chopped
- 1 inch fresh ginger root, grated
- 1 tbsp peanut or coconut oil
- 1 tbsp brown sugar
- 1 tsp shrimp paste
- ⅔ cup / 3½ oz unsalted peanuts, chopped
- ⅔ cup / 5¼ fl oz coconut milk
- 2 x 8 oz blocks of tempeh, cut into sticks
- 2 red onions, thinly sliced
- ½ cup / 4 fl oz mayonnaise

STEP 1

First, prepare a peanut sauce on the stove top. Cook the chili pepper, garlic, and ginger in the oil to soften without browning. Add the brown sugar, shrimp paste, and peanuts, then briefly fry. Pour in the coconut milk and simmer for 10 minutes. Remove from heat, and process the peanut sauce in the food processor to the desired consistency.

STEP 2

Preheat the air fryer to 400°F. Bake the tempeh, in batches if needed, until crispy, about 5–6 minutes. Toss halfway through cooking.

STEP 3

Divide the tempeh fries between four bowls, and serve with the peanut sauce, mayonnaise, and garnish with red onion rings.

jalapeño poppers
with cream cheese filling

INGREDIENTS TO SERVE 4

- ½ cup / 4 oz cream cheese
- salt and pepper, to taste
- 8 large red or green peppers, halved and de-seeded
- ¼ cup cornflakes
- ¼ cup panko
- ½ cup / 4 fl oz buttermilk
- 2 tbsp flour

You can bake almost anything in the air fryer to get that perfectly crispy crust. Coating food in breadcrumbs will give you the best result, but you can also get creative by using, for instance, finely ground cornflakes or tortilla chips, almond flour, other ground nuts, and grated coconut.

STEP 1

Lightly beat the cream cheese, season with salt and pepper, then stuff the pepper halves with the cream cheese. Finely grind the cornflakes and panko in the food processor to combine. Dip the stuffed peppers into the buttermilk, and coat in flour. Dip again into the buttermilk, then coat in the cornflake-panko mixture.

STEP 2

Preheat the air fryer to 350°F. Place a batch of the peppers in the air fryer basket. Bake in batches for 8–12 minutes until golden brown and crispy.

VARIATION

Stuff the peppers with herb cream cheese or cheddar cheese.

i love
your
sweet
dreams

Dessert

yogurt cake
with blueberries

INGREDIENTS FOR
1 LARGE OR 2 SMALL CAKES

- ⅔ cup / 5¼ oz butter
- 1 cup sugar
- 2 eggs
- ½ cup Greek yogurt
- 1 tbsp lemon zest
- 1 tsp vanilla extract
- 1¾ cups self-rising flour
- 1 cup fresh blueberries, plus extra for garnish
- powdered sugar, for dusting

STEP 1

Melt the butter in a saucepan on the stove top or in the microwave. Using a mixer, beat together the butter, sugar, eggs, yogurt, lemon zest, and vanilla extract until well blended. Sift the flour over the batter and fold together until combined. Fold in the blueberries.

Preheat the air fryer to 300°F. Grease a baking pan that fits into the air fryer, and line the bottom with parchment paper. Spoon the batter into the pan. Depending on the air fryer's capacity, you may fill 2 smaller pans. Smooth the surface, and bake the cake in the air fryer for 50 minutes.

STEP 2

Prick the cake with a skewer. If it comes out clean, the cake is done. Allow the cake to cool in the pan for 10 minutes, then turn it out onto a wire rack and allow to cool down completely. Sprinkle the cake with powdered sugar and garnish with the remaining blueberries.

cherry clafoutis

INGREDIENTS TO MAKE 1

- 1 cup cherries (about 21), pitted
- ¼ cup / 2 fl oz amaretto
- ½ cup self-rising flour
- 2 tbsp sugar
- pinch of salt
- 1 egg
- ½ cup / 4 fl oz crème fraîche
- 1 tbsp / 2 oz butter, cut into chunks
- powdered sugar

STEP 1

Combine the cherries in a bowl with the amaretto. In another bowl, mix the self-rising flour, sugar, salt, egg, and crème fraîche, and beat until a smooth and firm batter forms. Add a dash of water, if needed.

STEP 2

Preheat the air fryer to 350°F. Grease a tart pan that fits into the air fryer, and pour in the batter. Arrange the cherries over the batter and top with the butter chunks. Place the pan in the air fryer, and bake for 25 minutes, until golden brown.

STEP 3

Sprinkle the clafoutis generously with powdered sugar directly after baking.

VARIATION

Divide the cherries and batter into 4 smaller ramekins to make individual servings.

apple pie

INGREDIENTS FOR
1 LARGE OR 2 SMALL PIES

for the dough

- ½ cup / 4½ oz butter
- ⅔ cup sugar
- 1 tsp lemon zest
- pinch of salt
- 2 cups self-rising flour

for the filling

- 2 lb slightly sour apples (about 6, such as Jonagold, Golden Delicious, or Pink Lady), peeled and sliced
- ½ cup raisins
- pinch of ground cinnamon
- 1 cup sugar

STEP 1

Cut the butter together with the sugar, lemon zest, and a pinch of salt. Knead together until the mixture forms a dough. Cover the dough in plastic wrap, and refrigerate. Mix together the apples, raisins, ground cinnamon, and sugar, stirring to combine.

STEP 2

Take the dough out of the fridge. Roll out to the size of a pie pan that fits into the air fryer. Depending on the air fryer's capacity, you can make 2 apple pies with the dough. Grease the pie pan, and place the dough in the pan. Firmly press the bottom and edges. Prick holes in the bottom with a fork.

STEP 3

Preheat the air fryer to 325°F. Distribute the filling over the bottom. If you like, you can arrange dough strips over the filled pie. Place the pie pan in the air fryer basket, and bake the pie for 50 minutes. Allow to cool in the pan before serving.

sticky brownies

with almonds and salted caramel

INGREDIENTS TO MAKE 12–16

for the brownies

- 1 tbsp flour
- 2⅓ oz dark chocolate, broken into chunks
- 4½ tbsp / 2¼ oz butter
- 1 egg
- pinch of salt
- ¼ cup sugar
- ¼ cup brown sugar
- 1½ tsp vanilla extract
- ½ cup self-rising flour
- ¾ cup sliced almonds

for the salted caramel

- 1 cup sugar
- 7 tbsp / 3½ oz butter, cut into chunks
- ½ cup / 4 fl oz heavy cream
- 1 tsp coarse sea salt

STEP 1

Grease the sides of a baking pan that fits in the air fryer, and sprinkle with flour. Place a sheet of parchment paper on the bottom of the pan, and grease the sheet. Gently melt the chocolate with the butter in a double boiler. Beat together the egg, sugars, and a pinch of salt until light and fluffy. Gently fold in the melted chocolate. Add the flour and ½ cup almonds, stirring until a smooth batter forms.

Preheat the air fryer to 325°F. Spoon the batter into the baking pan. Smooth the surface, and bake in the air fryer for 25–30 minutes. Leaving the brownie in the pan, loosen the edges and transfer to a wire rack. Allow to cool, then cut into pieces.

STEP 2

To prepare the salted caramel, heat the sugar with ¼ cup / 2 fl oz water in a heavy-bottomed saucepan over medium heat, until the sugar is completely melted. Leave the sugar mixture to simmer. Do not stir, but swirl the pan occasionally. As the sugar begins to brown, gradually add the butter over low heat. Allow the butter to melt, then gradually add the cream, still over low heat. Briefly bring to a boil, then simmer for 1 minute. Remove the caramel from heat, and stir in the salt. Allow the caramel to cool.

STEP 3

Sprinkle the brownies with the rest of the almonds, and drizzle with the salted caramel.

apple roses
with lemon curd filling

INGREDIENTS TO MAKE 12

for the lemon curd

- zest and juice of 2 limes
- ½ cup superfine sugar
- 5 tablespoons / 2½ oz butter
- 2 eggs

for the apple roses

- 4 cups / 32 fl oz water
- 3 tbsp sugar
- 2 tbsp lemon juice
- 6 red apples, cut into ⅛-inch thick slices
- 12 puff pastry sheets, thawed, and cut into strips that measure about 2½ x 10 inches
- 2 tbsp powdered sugar

STEP 1

Bring the lime zest and juice, superfine sugar, and butter to a boil in a double boiler on the stove top, stirring until the sugar has dissolved. Leave the mixture to simmer for 3 minutes, stirring occasionally. Beat in the eggs, still in a double boiler, and keep stirring until the mixture thickens. Remove the pan from heat and allow the lemon curd to cool down completely.

STEP 2

Bring the water with sugar and lemon juice to a boil on the stove top. Put the apple slices in the boiling water and cook for 2 minutes until they are soft enough to bend. Drain well and allow to cool. Spread lemon curd on each strip of pastry dough, and arrange the apple slices along one long edge. Fold the bottom of the dough over the apple slices. Starting from one short end, roll up the dough so it forms a spiral with no gaps. Avoid rolling too tightly, or the apples may begin to slide out of the folded dough.

STEP 3

Preheat the air fryer to 400°F. Place a sheet of parchment paper on the bottom of the basket and place 3 to 4 roses on top. Bake the apple roses in the air fryer for 15–20 minutes, then remove and place on a wire rack to cool. Bake the remaining apple roses the same way. Sprinkle with powdered sugar just before serving.

Index

This edition published by Cottage Door Press, LLC, in 2019.
First published 2019 by ImageBooks, Veghel (NL).

5005 Newport Drive, Rolling Meadows, Illinois 60008

Recipes and food styling: Dorien Holla, Van de Kook
Additional recipes: Floor van Dinteren, Floorabella
Photography: Edgar van de Ven
Design by Studio ImageBooks
The cover shows Roast Beef with Herbed Potatoes (107).

ISBN: 978-1-68052-905-0

Printed in China

Love Food™ is an imprint of Cottage Door Press, LLC.
Parragon Books® and the Parragon® logo are registered trademarks of Cottage Door Press, LLC.

Notes for the Reader

This book uses standard kitchen measuring spoons and cups. All spoon and cup measurements are level unless otherwise indicated. Unless otherwise stated, milk is assumed to be whole, eggs are large, individual vegetables are medium, and pepper is freshly ground black pepper. Unless otherwise stated, all root vegetables should be peeled prior to using. People with nut allergies should be aware that some of the prepared ingredients used in the recipes in this book may contain nuts.

Garnishes, decorations, and serving suggestions are all optional and not necessarily included in the recipe ingredients or method. The times given are only an approximate guide. Preparation times differ according to the techniques used by different people and the cooking times may also vary from those given. Optional ingredients, variations, or serving suggestions have not been included in the time calculations.